Conforming Inspiration

EMBRACING YOUR UNIQUE DESIGN AND FINDING INNER BLISS ON A 7-STEP TRANSFORMATIONAL PATHWAY TO BEING BLISSFULLY UNIQUE

RENEE BLISS

Contents

The Path to Fulfillment

How Seeking Bliss in Authenticity Changes Lives One Person at a Time

I truly believe that self-love and acceptance are the secrets to living a fulfilled and happy life.

I know firsthand the struggle of trying to fit into a mold that wasn't meant for me.

It took me years of self-discovery and inner work to finally embrace my uniqueness and find my inner bliss.

And now, I am passionate about helping others do the same.

I personally know the weight of family, friends, and societal expectations all too well. The suffocating pressure to conform, to suppress my true self, and to blend in with the crowd. It's disheartening to witness so many of us, including myself, stifling our uniqueness for the sake of acceptance.

In today's society, the pressure to conform to the comparison trap perpetuated by social media can be overwhelming. It's no wonder that so many people feel disconnected from their true selves and struggle to find fulfillment in their lives.

The constant barrage of unrealistic beauty standards and the culture of perfectionism only add fuel to the fire, leading to feelings of inadequacy and low self-worth.

I refuse to let societal pressure and lack of self-love define me. I have made a conscious effort to realign my life, setting healthy boundaries and incorporating practices like prayer, meditation, and mindfulness into my daily routine.

It was a journey of courage, perseverance, and determination, and it ultimately led me to become a Certified Spiritual Life Coach.

As a Certified Spiritual Life Coach, I am passionate about helping others release their pain, trauma, and emotional baggage and embrace their uniqueness.

I have discovered that the roots of these issues run deep, with core values and beliefs being imprinted upon us from a young age, shaping how we view ourselves and the world around us.

Now that I have a deeper understanding and appreciation, I feel a deep desire to bring awareness to these issues and help others release their trauma and pain.

Furthermore, I am passionate about laying a strong foundation for self-love and self-acceptance in children so they can grow up embracing their unique design and finding their true inner bliss, which is essential for their growth into confident and content adults.

We all face countless challenges and obstacles when it comes to embracing our uniqueness and finding inner bliss, whether it's fear of judgment, feelings of inadequacy, or internalized messages of unworthiness.

I am enthusiastic to help individuals navigate these struggles and come out on the other side with a greater sense of self-confidence and self-acceptance.

This passionate and purposeful journey led me to found Blissful Trendz; it serves as a supportive platform for unique individuals to celebrate their distinctiveness without fear of judgment.

In a world where conformity is often praised, this business serves as a beacon of encouragement, reminding people that their uniqueness is their power.

It allows you to shine authentically, fostering deeper connections with others while bringing fresh perspectives to your personal and professional life.

You have the power to create a life that is uniquely yours, filled with joy, purpose, and an unshakable connection to the universe, and experience a higher spiritual awareness.

So, here's why embracing your unique design and finding inner bliss is important:

Embracing your unique design allows you to express your individuality and creativity, cultivating a sense of empowerment and self-confidence.

When you embrace your own unique style, you're telling the world that you are not afraid to stand out and be different.

This sense of empowerment can have a positive impact on all aspects of your life, from your personal relationships to your professional endeavors.

Finding inner bliss through embracing your unique design leads to a deeper understanding and acceptance of who you are, creating a stronger sense of self-awareness and fulfillment.

When you allow yourself to be true to your own style and preferences, you are effectively embracing your authentic self.

This self-awareness allows you to connect with your innermost desires and live a life that is true to your heart.

This newfound freedom allows you to express yourself in a way that is true to your beliefs and values.

Blissful Reflection:

Craftsman's Unique Lenses - Discover the Hidden Depths Within

In the bustling marketplace, a master craftsman showcased his skill in creating unique lenses for eyeglasses. Each lens was meticulously crafted and adorned with intricate, one-of-a-kind designs and colors.

People marveled at the breathtaking array of lenses, each capturing the essence of individuality and creativity.

A curious traveler approached the craftsman one day and asked, "Why do you create such diverse and unconventional lenses rather than sticking to one standard design?"

The wise craftsman smiled and replied, "Dear traveler, the world is a kaleidoscope of personalities, each person's journey filled with distinct colors and patterns."

Just as no two lenses are the same, no two individuals are identical. Our one-of-a-kind eyes see the world through a lens that is uniquely ours.

As the traveler pondered the craftsman's words, he remembered the verse from Proverbs 20:5 NIV—

> "The purposes of a person's heart are deep waters, but one who has insight draws them out."

He realized that just like the diverse lenses, each person holds their own depth, purpose, and wisdom within their hearts, waiting to be discovered.

The diverse lenses remind us that embracing our quirky individuality and acknowledging our unique purpose in the universe's grand design is a gift.

Just as the craftsman celebrates the diversity of his lenses, so too does our creator celebrate the diversity of each individual.

Our one-of-a-kind eyes remind us of our unparalleled place in the world, offering a remarkable perspective that contributes to the vibrant tapestry of humanity.

As we journey through life, may we appreciate the diverse lenses through which we view the world, cherishing our own uniqueness and embracing the individuality of others.

In doing so, we unveil the extraordinary wisdom and counsel that lies within us, recognizing our profound connection to His greater plan.

The craftsman's words lingered in the traveler's mind as he continued on his journey. He began to see the world in a different light, noticing the distinct beauty in people's individuality, just like the unique lenses the craftsman created.

He embraced the idea of drawing out the purpose and potential in others, understanding that everyone has something special to offer.

This newfound understanding led the traveler to help others recognize their own unique gifts and talents.

He became a mentor and guide, encouraging people to embrace their individuality and use it to impact the world positively.

As he did so, he found fulfillment and joy in seeing others thrive and succeed, knowing that he had played a part in drawing out their inner wisdom and purpose.

As we journey through life, may we appreciate the diverse lenses through which we view the world, cherishing our own uniqueness and embracing the individuality of others.

In doing so, we welcome the extraordinary wisdom and counsel that lies within us, recognizing our profound connection to His greater plan.

We all have depths within us, waiting to be explored and understood.

When we seek to truly understand others, we can draw out their purpose and potential. Let's strive to be people of understanding, ready to listen and uncover the hidden treasures within one another.

> "Whoever believes in me, as Scripture has said, rivers of living water will flow from within them." — John 7:38 NIV

Believing in the power of the spirit brings forth a wellspring of life, overflowing with vitality and renewal.

Just as a river nourishes and sustains the land, our faith has the power to revitalize and enrich our own lives and the lives of those around us.

Let's embrace this abundant flow of living water, allowing it to bring joy and fulfillment to our hearts and the hearts of others.

Now that we've explored the path to fulfillment, it's time to break free from conformity and chart our own path to happiness and fulfillment.

Breaking Free from Conformity

THE ULTIMATE GUIDE TO EMBRACING YOUR UNWAVERING INDIVIDUALITY

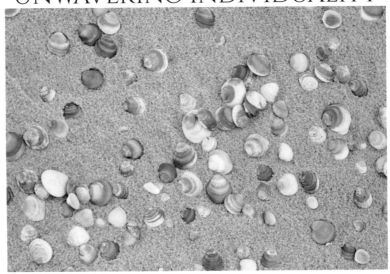

"Follow your bliss, and the universe will open doors for you where there were only walls." – Joseph Campbell

Embracing your unique design and finding inner bliss is not just about following a set of steps - it's about understanding and accepting yourself at a deep level.

It's about acknowledging that you are unlike anyone else, and that is your greatest strength.

The 7-step transformational pathway outlined in this book is designed to guide you on a journey of self-discovery, empowerment, and spiritual awakening.

It is a roadmap to help you break free from the constraints of conformity and societal expectations, and to embrace a life that is authentically yours.

Each main step in this process is carefully designed to help you tap into your innate potential and connect with your true purpose.

By reflecting on your passions, values, and moments of joy, you begin to uncover the unique design that sets you apart.

Releasing yourself from the burden of conformity and expectations is a crucial step in reclaiming your individuality and choosing your own path.

You will learn to cultivate daily joy and purpose, and deepen your connection to the universe.

Aligning your actions with your inner bliss and purpose, and embracing challenges as opportunities for growth, requires resilience, self-trust, and a positive mindset.

This pathway is ultimately about not only finding inner bliss and fulfillment for yourself, but also sharing your unique design with the world.

You become a source of inspiration and hope for others, creating a supportive and inclusive community that celebrates individuality and self-expression.

<u>**Blissful Reflection:**</u>

Uncover the Hidden Wisdom of the Seashells and Embrace Your Unique Story

Along the sandy strands of a small coastal town, each incoming tide graced the earth with a mosaic of seashells.

These fragments of marine life, with their spirals and hues, serve as whispered tales from a world beneath waves, each a former home to creatures of the sea.

Just like these shells, every person holds within them a story spun by the yarn of their experience — unique, intricate, and altogether remarkable.

They are but physical reminders that within the ocean's embrace lies a spectrum of life as varied and colorful as the human experience itself.

If one dares to listen, the shells speak of journeys through uncharted waters, and storms weathered, much like our own paths through life.

The whispering roars of the ocean hidden within a shell's curve mirror the less tangible, but no less powerful, currents that move within the human heart.

> Proverbs 20:5 NIV — "The purposes of a person's heart are deep waters, but one who has insight draws them out."

conveys these inner streams to deep water, suggesting that wisdom resides in those depths, available to those who seek it.

As shells are the ocean's memoirs, so are our own insights and revelations buried beneath the surface of our immediate perception, awaiting the patient explorer to unearth them.

The gentle ceaseless lapping of the sea is similar to the persistence we must adopt in our quest for self-discovery.

As we examine the granules of our lives to find the pearls of insight, we must remember that the ocean itself does not yield its treasures easily.

It is a patient hand and a discerning eye that will coax the wisdom from the heart, finding truth in places unlooked for, much as one stumbles upon a perfect shell half-buried in the sand.

Yet this quiet quest is not without its strife. In the serene setting of the coastal town, hearts beat in quiet turmoil, constrained by societal molds and buried under the weight of imposed expectations.

The struggle for authenticity is not unlike the shelled creatures that outgrow their homes and must venture forth to find another.

Humans, too, must shed the encumbering layers to live as their true selves, transcending the facades that life often demands.

In this struggle, a soothing voice can sometimes break through the disharmony of conflicting desires and pressures.

It is the voice of our own inner wisdom, counseling us to thirst for the spring of spiritual awareness that can quench our deepest yearnings.

It calls us to embrace the unique contours of our spirit, to find our joy and purpose, and to discover our place within the interconnected web of existence.

This awakening often starts with understanding the true essence of conformity. In its ancient use within the Biblical context, *'Syschematizo'* hinted at a metamorphosis of one's nature, a transformation from within with outward manifestations.

The challenge, then, as supported by Romans 12:2 NKJV —

"And do not be conformed to this world, but be transformed
by the renewing of your mind, that you may prove what *is* that
good and acceptable and perfect will of God."

is not a superficial blending with the environment but an inner revolution that redefines one's interfaces with the world.

It is this choice — conformity versus transformation — that defines our journey.

So, embracing this profound change, individuals in the seaside town began their individual metamorphoses.

Their lives blossomed into vibrant representations of human diversity and strength.

No longer mere reflections of one another, they became testaments to personal evolution and the unwavering spirit's journey toward wholeness and authenticity.

Refreshed by the oceans of their own wisdom and resilience, they emerged from the pressures that had once encased them like the mollusks within their shells.

They began sharing narratives of hope and the rich diversity of the human condition with newfound freedom.

No longer adrift on the sea of expectations, they navigated their courses with the compass of self-knowledge and the map of their distinctive truths.

The seashells lying along the shore, with their myriad forms and pigments, seek to remind us of the ocean's captivating artistry.

Every contour, every color tells of the sea's ability to nurture life in all its wondrous forms.

They inspire us to recognize and appreciate the scope of beauty and complexity in the depths of the ocean.

Likewise, every individual constitutes a living symbol of the astonishing array found within humanity.

Each with their distinct journey, they collectively testify to the infinite expressions of life, strength, and the enduring allure of the human spirit.

Like the countless shells upon the beach, our lives, when viewed as a whole, represent the rainbow-like tapestry woven by the countless hues of our experiences.

Like the seashells on the shore, we have to go deep to seek the wisdom within ourselves.

Those hidden stories that, when unearthed and honored, reveal the full breadth of our potential.

It's an invitation to stroll along the beaches of our souls, to gather our unique shells, and to display proudly the beauty of our personal journeys for the world to witness, as we stride forth into life's vast, unending oceans.

Now that we've learned the importance of breaking free from conformity, it's time to delve deeper into the beauty of our quirky individuality.

Embracing Your Quirky Individuality

YOUR ONE-OF-A-KIND DESIGN AND PURPOSE

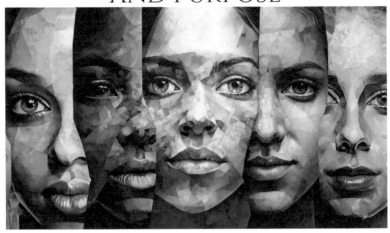

E ach of us is made unique and special, down to the very details of our eyes. Just as no two pairs of eyes are the same, no two souls are alike. Embrace your quirks and individuality, for they are a reflection of your one-of-a-kind design and purpose.

- Reflect on your passions, talents, and values to gain a deeper understanding of what makes you uniquely you.

- Identify moments of fulfillment and joy in your life to provide valuable insights into your true purpose and unique design.

- Explore your personal strengths and qualities to align with your authentic self and live a more purposeful life.

- Seek guidance from mentors or spiritual leaders who can offer insight and wisdom as you navigate your journey of self-discovery.

- Embrace your individuality and authenticity, honoring your true self and opening yourself up to living a life filled with joy, purpose, and connection.

Blissful Reflection:

How a Village Learned to Celebrate Their One-Of-A-Kind Design and Purpose

Once, there was a young woman named Eliza, a resident of a village as picturesque as a painter's masterpiece.

Her eyes were a marvel—a blue that rivaled the expansiveness of the sky on a cloudless day, scattered with flickers of light evocative of the distant stars.

And yet, despite the obvious beauty, a weight rested upon Eliza's heart.

She wished not for eyes that spoke of oceans and night skies but for ones that whispered of normalcy, for to be ordinary seemed far easier than to bear the burden of standing out.

Amid the fabric of her daily life, woven with threads of self-doubt, Eliza chanced upon an old woman, whose aura seemed composed of the very wisdom of the ages.

A single glance was all it took for the elderly sage to read Eliza's heart, and with a smile steeped in the warmth of a thousand suns, she began to tell a tale.

This story spoke not of ordinary men and women but of a King whose hands shaped the cosmos with loving precision.

Particularly, it was the appearance of each individual that received the touch of the King's grand design.

Quoting from the ancient text of Psalm 139:14 NKJV—

"I will praise You, for I am fearfully *and* wonderfully made;
Marvelous are Your works, And *that* my soul knows very well."

the old woman reminded Eliza. It was a message of intentional uniqueness, of divine joy in the singular beauty of every creation.

Within Eliza, the words of the wise woman began their transformative dance, twirling and spinning her perspective into a new pattern.

The ocean, in her eyes, was no longer a cause for shame but rather a miraculous work of the divine hand, designed with intention and love.

Eliza's eyes, once a source of disquiet, now became beacons of her distinctness and purpose.

She found further solace and inspiration in another piece of scripture, Ephesians 2:10 NIV, which reads,

> "For we are God's handiwork, created in Christ Jesus to do
> good works, which God prepared in advance for us to do."

This promised that her uniqueness was not an accident, but that there existed a preordained path, etched by the divine for her to tread.

As Eliza traversed the village lanes anew, her once downcast gaze now sought the faces of those she met.

The incredible array of eyes that met hers became a canvas of countless stories, each a testament to the King's infinite creativity and love.

No longer did she see a crowd from which she wished to hide, but a kaleidoscope of spirits, none identical, all cherished.

Her revelation was contagious, and soon, the hearts of the villagers began to pulsate to the rhythm of Psalm 139:14 NKJV —

> "I will praise You, for I am fearfully *and* wonderfully made;
> Marvelous are Your works, And *that* my soul knows very well."

They wrapped themselves in the comfort that they were made with divine care, each a distinct thread in an intricate tapestry.

With unveiled pride in their design and destiny, they flourished, basking in the joy of self-acceptance.

The very essence of the village transmuted as Eliza's story touched the hearts of the people.

Where once they strode, eyes downcast, hoping not to stir the seas of conformity, they now paraded with a resolve, the fire of purpose igniting the sparkle in their eyes, each a signature of the King's loving precision.

The villagers came together in their newfound authenticity, a community where the magnificence of every soul's design was celebrated.

Their differences were not just tolerated but revered as tangible manifestations of divine intent. In this harmonious existence, they often turned to Jeremiah 1:5 NIV as a manifesto:

> "Before I formed you in the womb I knew you, before you were born, I set you apart; I appointed you as a prophet to the nations."

Eliza and her fellows no longer merely existed; they thrived, as if each day was a fresh canvas on which to paint their truth.

They became a living embodiment of 1 Peter 4:10 NIV, which urges,

> "Each of you should use whatever gift you have received to serve others, as faithful stewards of God's grace in its various forms."

Their village was a testament, living proof that individuality is not a roadblock but a highway to fulfillment.

In culmination, Eliza's village was transformed into a beacon of hope amidst the rolling hills.

Here, Romans 12:6-8 NIV—

> "We have different gifts, according to the grace given to each of us. If your gift is prophesying, then prophesy in accordance with your faith; if it is serving, then serve; if it is teaching, then teach; if it is to encourage, then give encouragement; if it is giving, then give generously; if it is to lead, do it diligently; if it is to show mercy, do it cheerfully."

was not just scripture but a way of life, empowering each villager to serve and thrive in accordance with their God-given abilities.

This story of Eliza and her remarkable eyes implores us to recognize the unique beauty within each of us, to embrace the distinct gifts bestowed upon us, and to courageously fulfill our divine purpose amidst humanity's endlessly diverse spectrum.

Understanding and embracing your individuality is essential for living a truly fulfilling and authentic life.

When you acknowledge and honor your unique qualities, passions, and perspectives, you are able to create a life that is entirely your own.

This means pursuing your interests, following your own path, and being true to yourself.

The journey to self-discovery is one of the most beautiful experiences life offers, allowing us to explore the depths of our being and the world around us.

When you embrace who you are, you not only empower yourself to make decisions that resonate deeply with your innermost desires but also pave the way for a life rich with self-expression.

By doing so, you can experience a deep sense of joy, purpose, and fulfillment that comes from living in alignment with who you are at your core.

Remember, every step taken in authenticity is a step towards a life of enriched experiences, connections, and accomplishments that truly reflect the essence of your spirit.

When you are fully in tune with your authentic self, you can better tap into the wisdom and guidance of the universe.

This alignment can usher in a deeper understanding of your purpose in life, as well as a greater sense of peace and clarity.

It's similar to finding your own frequency in the symphony of life and playing it with courage and conviction.

To truly embrace your individuality, it's important to celebrate and express your unique qualities and gifts.

This could involve pursuing creative passions, sharing your thoughts and ideas with others, or simply being unapologetically yourself in all areas of your life.

By doing this, you can inspire others to embrace their own individuality and create a ripple effect of authenticity and empowerment throughout the world.

The brilliance of your individual light can be a beacon for those lost in conformity, illuminating paths to self-acceptance and courage.

In a world that often seeks to fit us into boxes, your unwavering commitment to your individuality is not just a personal triumph, but a collective gift.

So, go ahead, embrace your individuality, and shine your light brightly for all to see – the world is waiting!

Let's dive into the steps to embracing your quirky individuality!

Step 1: Reflect On Your Passions, Talents, and Values

Embracing your quirky individuality isn't just about self-acceptance; it's an empowering journey toward self-discovery and fulfillment.

Each of us carries a symphony of passions, talents, and values that, like a fingerprint, are ours alone.

When you wholeheartedly embrace who you are, you cast a light on the unique gifts and abilities that distinguish you from the rest.

This self-embrace is not simply about acknowledging what sets you apart - it's about celebrating it!

By understanding and valuing your quirks and individual nature, you position yourself to live in harmony with your core being, crafting a life narrative that is richly authentic.

Such authenticity serves as the cornerstone for a life of deep contentment and purpose, one that isn't dictated by societal templates but illuminated by your own personal truths and aspirations.

Taking pride in your quirky individuality, you navigate the world with a beacon that uncovers what truly enlivens your spirit and ignites your passion.

Your unusual humor, your unconventional style, your idiosyncratic thought processes—these are not abnormalities to be hidden, but gems to be polished and showcased.

In a society that often promotes conformity, your distinctiveness is a breath of fresh air, adding color and texture to the tapestry of life.

Embracing this distinctive flair can transform everyday experiences into adventures and routines into originality.

As you learn to love your quirks, you'll discover a profound source of joy and excitement rooted in the genuine self-expression of what makes you, unmistakably, you.

In this celebration of individuality, you embark on a lifelong journey where passion and enthusiasm are your loyal companions, and where living as your true self is the greatest adventure of all.

<u>Here are some additional steps:</u>

Find a quiet, comfortable space to spend some uninterrupted time reflecting on your passions, talents, and values.

Grab a notebook or journal to jot down your thoughts and ideas as you reflect.

Close your eyes and take a few deep breaths to center yourself and clear your mind.

Think about the activities and hobbies that bring you the most joy and excitement. What are the things that you love to do in your free time?

Consider any talents or skills that come naturally to you. What are you good at? What do others often compliment you on?

Reflect on your values and beliefs. What principles are most important to you? What do you stand for, and what truly matters to you in life?

Write down any patterns or common themes that you notice in your reflections. Are there any recurring interests, talents, or values that stand out to you?

Consider how you can incorporate your passions, talents, and values into your daily life and work. How can you align your actions and decisions with what truly matters to you?

Think about how you can cultivate and nurture your passions, talents, and values. Can you pursue new opportunities or experiences to further develop and express them?

Take some time to appreciate and celebrate the unique person that you are, and remember to honor and prioritize your passions, talents, and values as you move forward in life.

Step 2: Identify Moments of Fulfillment and Joy in Your Life

By holding dear to these distinctive elements of your personality, you're not simply standing out; you're asserting your place in the world as an irreplaceable piece of the human puzzle.

Embracing your quirky individuality is similar to giving yourself permission to dance freely to the rhythm of your own life's music.

It's in this dance that your steps become your signature, impossible to replicate. When you live with this authenticity, you align with your deepest values, and everything you do feels resonant and true.

This harmony between self and action illuminates your path, guiding you toward your life's purpose, and ultimately, filling your days with a sense of fulfillment that is both rare and deeply rewarding.

As you traverse the valleys and peaks of your personal journey, take a moment to bask in the glow of the moments that have brought you unadulterated joy.

Pause to consider—what is the essence that made those instances stand out?

Perhaps it was the exhilarating sensation of breaking free from the shackles of expectation, the pride swelling in your chest from hard-earned triumphs, or maybe the warmth of profound connections forged through the raw showcasing of your true self.

Those flashes of bliss are beacons that highlight the power and joy of embracing your distinctive individuality.

They are a testament to the magnetic pull of authenticity and how it draws us toward our life's true north.

So, wear your quirks as a badge of honor, for they are the brushstrokes of your unique life portrait.

In living boldly and wholeheartedly as your most genuine self, you unlock the potential to discover and fulfill your destiny, finding a deeper contentment and carving a legacy defined by shameless originality and purposeful living.

Here are some additional steps:

Take time to reflect on your life and identify specific moments when you felt the most fulfilled and joyful.

Make a list of these moments and write down what you were doing during those times.

Consider the people who were with you during these moments and how they contributed to your feelings of fulfillment and joy.

Reflect on the impact these experiences had on you and how they shaped your perspective and values.

Think about the qualities or activities that were present during these moments and what made them so meaningful to you.

Consider how these moments align with your passions, strengths, and values.

Evaluate how these moments may provide clues about your true purpose and unique design.

Take note of any common themes or patterns that emerge from these moments of fulfillment and joy.

Consider how you can incorporate more of these activities or qualities into your daily life to create more moments of fulfillment and joy.

Use these insights to guide your future decisions and actions, and to cultivate a life that is aligned with your true purpose.

Step 3: Explore Your Personal Strengths and Qualities

In a society that often prizes a one-size-fits-all approach, summoning the courage to flaunt your unique hues and personal rhythm can be transformative.

You are a rich tapestry of unparalleled traits and idiosyncrasies that, when woven together, create a masterpiece of individuality that is uniquely yours.

Embracing this distinctiveness propels you beyond the realm of ordinary, fueling your journey with a vibrant authenticity that captivates and inspires.

Recognize and honor your peculiar quirks, for they are the brushstrokes of your personality, painting a portrait of self that is both extraordinary and intriguing.

When you leverage these traits across the depiction of life—professionally, personally, and in forging connections with others—you become an unstoppable force of originality, leaving an unforgettable mark of brilliance in your wake. Your eccentricities are not just accessories to your character; they are your superpowers.

Revel in them and watch as you illuminate the world.

Delight in your playful spirit, your offbeat humor, the uncommon paths of thought that meander through your mind—they are a testament to your extraordinary blueprint.

By fully acknowledging and nurturing your innate strengths and capabilities, you not only ascend toward the apex of self-realization but also radiate a beacon of inspiration for others to unearth and celebrate their own distinctiveness.

Picture yourself as a gardener, where your special traits are like rare and exotic flowers amidst a field of common blooms.

Cultivate them with care, and they will flourish, bringing joy, color, and fragrance not just to your own life but to the lives of those who cross your path.

Your journey is more than mere existence; it's a quest to imprint this world with the unmistakable signature of your soul.

As you step into the sunlight of your true essence, remember that your individuality is not just a privilege—it's a gift to society that beckons for the touch of originality that only you can provide.

Celebrate yourself, for in doing so, you're not just embracing quirks—you're embarking on a legacy.

<u>Here are some additional steps:</u>

Reflect on past successes and achievements to identify your personal strengths and qualities.

Ask for feedback from friends, family, and colleagues to gain a better understanding of how others perceive your strengths.

Use self-assessment tools, such as personality tests or strength assessments, to pinpoint your unique qualities.

Spend time doing activities that bring you joy and fulfillment, as these often align with your natural strengths.

Seek out experiences that challenge you and provide opportunities to showcase your strengths.

Keep a journal or log of experiences where you excel or feel especially confident to help identify recurring strengths.

Take note of the qualities you admire in others, as these can provide insight into your own strengths and values.

Seek out mentorship or coaching to gain guidance on how to leverage your strengths for personal and professional growth.

Reflect on how your strengths can be applied in different areas of your life, such as career, relationships, and personal development.

Embrace and celebrate your strengths, recognizing that they make you uniquely capable and valuable.

Step 4: Seek Guidance from Mentors or Spiritual Leaders

Embracing your quirky individuality is like unfolding a map to a hidden treasure—the genuine essence of who you are.

In this journey, mentors and spiritual leaders serve as wise navigators, guiding you through the terrains of self-discovery with their well-traveled insights.

They are lighthouses in a fog of conformity, illuminating paths of self-acceptance that you may not have braved alone.

When you consult with these seasoned souls, it isn't just their knowledge that benefits you, but also the sharing of their personal journeys.

This confluence of experience and authenticity ignites inspiration, helping you to recognize the beauty in your quirks and idiosyncrasies.

Such guidance is less about altering your course to fit the mold and more about charting a course that honors your unique blueprint—the personal anecdotes and wisdom they offer foster a deep appreciation for your own individual design and purpose.

Every quirk you possess is a thread in the vibrant tapestry of your being, and mentors, along with spiritual leaders, are there to encourage you to weave these threads with both courage and joy.

Their advice extends beyond the philosophical; it is grounded in the practicality of living authentically within a world that often prizes uniformity.

These guides are skilled at constructing a nurturing environment, rich with empathetic language and inclusive thought, giving you the freedom to express your individuality without fear of judgment.

As you venture towards full acceptance of your unique self, their supportive presence acts as a steadying hand—allowing you to celebrate your distinctions with confidence and pride.

Equipped with their balanced approach, you'll find that maintaining internal harmony and fostering positive relationships becomes second nature, despite the clamor of the world outside.

Follow their lead, and you'll learn that to live as your truest self is not just personal fulfillment, but also a gift to those around you, displaying the splendor of embracing a life unbound by sameness.

Here are some additional steps:

Consider your own beliefs and values to determine the type of mentor or spiritual leader you would like to seek guidance from.

Research potential mentors or spiritual leaders who have experience and wisdom in areas relevant to your journey.

Reach out to these individuals and express your interest in seeking their guidance.

Schedule a meeting or conversation to discuss your goals and seek their advice.

Be open and receptive to their insights and perspectives, even if they differ from your own.

Take notes and reflect on the guidance these mentors or spiritual leaders offer.

Consider implementing their advice into your decision-making process and actions.

Keep in regular contact with these individuals to seek ongoing guidance and support.

Express gratitude for their time and wisdom and show your willingness to learn and grow from their mentorship.

Pay it forward by offering your own guidance and support to others in need, creating a cycle of mentorship and spiritual leadership.

Step 5: Embrace Your Individuality and Authenticity

In an age where social media often dictates uniformity and conformity, daring to showcase your distinctive quirks and peculiarities is both revolutionary and empowering.

The distinctive rhythm of your laugh, the eccentric hobbies that ignite your passion, or the unique perspective you bring to a conversation—all of these aspects constitute the irreplaceable mosaic of your identity.

Embracing these traits is not merely an act of bold self-expression; it is an open invitation to the world to engage with the authentic essence of who you are.

By doing so, you not only contribute an original voice to the chorus of humanity but also carve out a space where others may feel encouraged to reveal their true selves.

Picture a world where each individual's unique talents and perspectives are not just recognized but celebrated—it starts with the courage to live proudly in the light of your own individuality, irrespective of the judgments or scrutiny that may come.

Your quirky individuality is the beacon that guides you towards a horizon of fulfillment and success that can only be reached on the untrodden path of authenticity.

The cost of fitting in—sacrificing your true self on the altar of social acceptance—is far too great in comparison to the unparalleled joy of living a life infused with your deepest truths and aspirations.

When you honor your personal oddities and strengths, you are not just building a life of personal satisfaction; you are also asserting that the qualities which differentiate you are not flaws but strengths, vital to the progression of innovation and diversity in the world.

Let us remember that history's most influential figures were those who dared to differ, to break molds, and to redefine the boundaries of possibility.

Embrace your individuality with pride and walk fearlessly into a future where your unique essence not only shapes your destiny but also illuminates the paths of those who have yet to discover the beauty of embracing their own exceptional nature.

Stand tall, stand out—be the irreplaceable you that the world not only desires but unequivocally needs.

<u>Here are some additional steps:</u>

Reflect on your strengths and weaknesses to better understand your individuality.

Identify the values and beliefs that are important to you and shape your authentic self.

Let go of societal expectations and judgments to embrace your true self without fear or shame.

Surround yourself with people who appreciate and support your individuality and authenticity.

Practice self-acceptance and self-love to build confidence in your unique qualities.

Take time to explore and express your passions and interests without conforming to societal norms.

Embrace your flaws and imperfections as part of what makes you authentically you.

Take risks and step outside of your comfort zone to show the world your true self.

Share your unique perspective and experiences with others to inspire and connect with like-minded individuals.

You are one-of-a-kind, and your journey to embracing your unique design and purpose is a beautiful and sacred process.

Embrace your individuality and authenticity, and you will unlock the true potential of your blissfully unique self.

Ways to be Fearlessly You:

Reflect on your unique qualities and what makes you different from others.

Accept that it's okay to be different and embrace your individuality.

Identify the things that make you feel most like yourself and bring you joy.

Surround yourself with people who appreciate and support your authenticity.

Practice self-compassion and celebrate your strengths and quirks.

Set boundaries to protect your authentic self from influences that may try to change you.

Take time to explore your interests and passions, and let them shape your identity.

Be open to trying new things and stepping out of your comfort zone to embrace your true self.

Embrace the journey of self-discovery and growth as you continue to embrace your individuality and authenticity.

Chapter Summary

- Reflect on your passions, talents, and values.

- Identify moments of fulfillment and joy in your life.

- Explore your personal strengths and qualities.

- Seek guidance from mentors or spiritual leaders.

- Embrace your individuality and authenticity.

FAQ:

What are some examples of passions, talents, and values that can help someone understand their unique design and purpose?

In today's society, it can be tempting to try and fit into a certain mold and suppress our individual quirks in order to be accepted by others.

However, embracing our unique individuality is crucial in understanding and fulfilling our one-of-a-kind design and purpose.

Each one of us possesses a combination of passions, talents, and values that shape our identity and set us apart from others.

It is essential to recognize and honor these unique traits, as they play a vital role in guiding us towards our purpose in life.

For example, someone who is passionate about environmental conservation may find their purpose in advocating for sustainable living or working towards creating a greener community.

Similarly, an individual with a talent for music may discover that their purpose lies in using their musical abilities to uplift and inspire others.

By embracing our quirky individuality and recognizing our passions, talents, and values, we gain a deeper understanding of our one-of-a-kind design and purpose.

This self-awareness allows us to live authentically and make a meaningful impact on the world around us.

It is important to remember that our quirks and idiosyncrasies are what make us special, and it is through embracing these traits that we can truly understand our purpose and design in this world.

How can identifying moments of fulfillment and joy in one's life help in understanding one's purpose and unique design?

Identifying moments of fulfillment and joy in our lives can provide important clues into our purpose and unique design.

When we pay attention to the activities, relationships, and experiences that bring us joy and fulfillment, we can start to notice patterns and themes that can guide us toward our true calling.

These moments represent moments when we are most aligned with our authentic selves, and often, they can provide a glimpse into the things that truly matter to us.

By embracing and celebrating these moments, we can gain valuable insight into our passions, strengths, and values, helping us to understand our purpose and design more clearly.

This self-awareness allows you to step into your unique design and purpose with confidence, knowing that you are living a life that is true to yourself.

Why is it important to seek guidance from mentors or spiritual leaders in understanding one's unique design and purpose?

These individuals often have a deep understanding of human nature and can help you recognize and embrace your quirky individuality.

By seeking their guidance, you can gain a fresh perspective on your strengths and weaknesses, and they can help you navigate the path toward fulfilling your one-of-a-kind purpose.

Furthermore, mentors and spiritual leaders can offer support and encouragement as you embrace your quirky individuality and strive to live out your unique design and purpose.

They can help you overcome any self-doubt or fear of judgment, and provide you with the tools and strategies to confidently express your authentic self.

Their guidance can empower you to embrace your individuality and stand out from the crowd, allowing you to make a meaningful impact in the world based on your own distinct strengths and talents.

With their help, you can truly understand and appreciate the value of being true to yourself and living a purpose-driven life.

What are some examples of unique strengths and qualities that someone might possess, and how can they help in understanding one's design and purpose?

Some examples of unique strengths and qualities that someone might possess include empathy, adaptability, creativity, analytical thinking, and leadership.

Empathy is a foundational trait that allows someone to connect with others on a deeper level. It's the ability to understand and share the feelings of another that can make a significant impact on personal and professional relationships.

Adaptability is another important strength to have, as it allows individuals to respond effectively to changing circumstances and thrive in diverse environments.

Being able to think on your feet and pivot when necessary is a valuable skill that can lead to success in various situations.

Creativity is a strength that can set someone apart in their field, allowing them to see things from new perspectives and come up with innovative solutions.

Analytical thinking is also beneficial, as it enables individuals to break down complex problems into manageable parts and make informed decisions.

Lastly, leadership is a quality that can inspire and motivate others, bringing out the best in a team and driving them toward a common goal.

These unique strengths and qualities aren't just valuable on an individual level but can also contribute to creating positive change in the world.

Now that we have celebrated our unique design and purpose, it's time to release ourselves from the weight of societal expectations. In the next chapter, we will explore how to shake off the "shoulds" and shed the burden of conformity, allowing our authentic selves to emerge and thrive.

Shaking Off the Shoulds

SHEDDING EXPECTATIONS AND CONFORMITY

"**B**e steadfast, immovable, always abounding in the work of the Lord, knowing that in the Lord your labor is not in vain." - 1 Corinthians 15:58 (ESV)

- Set boundaries with unsupportive individuals who impose their expectations on you, ensuring that you prioritize your well-being and unique design.

- Practice self-compassion and self-care, allowing you to prioritize your needs and cultivate a sense of inner peace and authenticity.

- Let go of societal pressures and judgments, empowering you to confidently embrace your uniqueness and worthiness without feeling inadequate.

- Surround yourself with positive and uplifting influences, creating a supportive environment that celebrates your uniqueness and empowers you to be true to yourself.

- Embrace your individuality and the right to choose your own path, giving you the confidence and empowerment to make decisions that align with your true self.

Blissful Reflection:

How One Ancient Oak Tree's Advice Changed a Forest Forever

Once upon a time, in a vast and vibrant forest, there reigned an ancient oak named Eli.

His time-worn bark bore the creases and grooves etched by countless years of weathering the elements.

So, too, were these scars symbolic of the wisdom he had accrued, the stories he could tell, and the courage he'd built throughout his enduring existence.

Amongst the youthful foliage, a green sapling by the name of Lily reached out to Eli with eyes full of aspirations.

She longed to match the grandeur and strength of both Eli and the forest's many towering giants.

Eli's raspy leaves rustled into a comforting smile as he prepared to impart his story, his words about to sow the seeds of inspiration.

Eli began his tale with a simple truth that laid within the intricate patterns of tree bark, each unique and irreplaceable, much like the soul of every individual. He drew from the timeless wisdom of Romans 12:2 NIV—

> "And do not be conformed to this world, but be transformed by the renewing of your mind, that you may prove what *is* that good and acceptable and perfect will of God."

urging Lily and all who would hear, to refrain from being molded by the fleeting desires of this world.

Instead, Eli advocated for a transformation through the renewal of the mind, a journey to discern God's will - a will that is good, pleasing, and perfect.

Eli's story was not simply a tale of growth; it was a call to recognize and realize the unique purpose and strength endowed by our Creator, a life not bound by the earthly measure but aligned with the divine.

As Lily found herself immersed in Eli's guidance, it was in letting go – like trees shedding leaves – that Eli urged her to strip away the expectations and pressures that others had placed upon her.

In another vibrant scripture, Galatians 5:1 NIV, Eli reiterated the gift of freedom,

> "It is for freedom that Christ has set us free. Stand firm, then, and do not let yourselves be burdened again by a yoke of slavery."

To cherish individuality is to embrace the strength and freedom that comes with it. Eli mapped out a path for Lily, a road paved by self-acceptance and liberation from the shackles of conformity.

Under Eli's mentorship, Lily learned the splendor of her oddities, her unique twists and turns similar to the glorious asymmetry of tree bark.

She learned to establish boundaries, to shower herself with kindness, and to nourish her spirit with wholesome company.

This mirrored the exhortation found in Colossians 3:23 NIV—

> "Whatever you do, work at it with all your heart, as working for the Lord, not for human masters,"

where every deed is a heartfelt offering to the Lord.

In her growth, both spiritual and physical, Lily wove this character into every fiber of her being.

As seasons passed, Lily flourished into a beacon of resilience and distinctiveness. Her roots deepened in self-awareness, and her branches reached skyward in confidence.

Her existence was no longer a silent echo of others' expectations but a resonant declaration of her own identity. She had unearthed an unshakeable joy and a drive that pulsed to the rhythm of God's grand design.

Her story unfolded, a banner of inspiration to the forest's youngest aspirants; it was a testament to the unconquerable spirit that lies within when one embraces their crafted uniqueness.

Lily's narrative went on to fuel a movement throughout the forest, kindling a fire in each young sapling to accept and honor their distinctiveness in the face of worldly molds.

Her legacy rippled across the woodland, as a catalyst for others to cast aside the mantle of uniformity and wear their quirks with pride.

Her life, once a quiet yearning for stature, had transformed into an anthem of individual triumph.

Lily became the embodiment of overcoming adversity, her story a narrative of strengthening one's core and flourishing against the odds.

She became a living inspiration for all of the forest's inhabitants to cherish their idiosyncrasies, and live true to their purpose, as Eli had illuminated for her.

The forest buzzed with newfound energy, as its community learned to value diversity and tenacity, just as each tree's bark was uniquely its own.

The forest landscape transformed, and with it, the hearts of its inhabitants.

A culture of honor for the inherent differences among them blossomed, and what was once a mere collection of trees had become a sanctuary of hope, determination, and boundless potential.

Their shared journey towards self-discovery and growth had been etched into the forest's history, much like the varied patterns etched into their bark.

It had all begun with Eli, the venerable oak, whose rugged exterior was a living testimony to the life-altering power of embracing one's quirks and aligning with God's greater vision.

His wisdom, like sunlight through the canopy, brought growth and clarity to those who sought meaning beyond the mundane - a reminder of the beauty that lies in one's God-given distinctive makeup.

As we reflect upon Lily's transformation, two scriptures bring our tale into sharp focus.

First is Galatians 1:10 NIV—

"Am I now trying to win the approval of human beings,
or of God? Or am I trying to please people? If I were still trying
to please people, I would not be a servant of Christ."

which questions the pursuit of human approval over divine service.

This verse thunders a resounding message — To become true servants of Christ, we must rise above our desire to please others.

Next, Proverbs 29:25 NIV—

"Fear of man will prove to be a snare, but whoever trusts in the Lord is kept safe."

offers a telling contrast between the ensnarement by fear of man and the sanctuary found in trusting the Lord.

This wisdom casts a shield of safety, an armor against the trepidation of human judgment.

In the dance of life echoed by the rustling forest leaves, these scriptures resonate with the call to live a story written by the Master's hand, where the joy and purpose we find are but fragments of the greater masterpiece he has designed.

Through the tale of Lily and the guidance of Eli, we are reminded that our existence is a canvas for the divine, and in honoring our quirks and heeding His call, we find strength, fulfillment, and our place within the eternal tapestry of His wondrous plan.

The chains of conformity bind many of us, bound by countless "shoulds" that determine our decisions and forge our paths.

To unlock the shackles of societal expectations, it is imperative to hold a mirror to our lives and ask the piercing question: "Am I cultivating my garden, or am I merely tending to someone else's?"

This interrogation of self requires courage, for it may lead us down an uncharted course, away from the well-paved roads of conformity.

Scrutinize the norms you've been told to uphold, the roles you've been instructed to fill, and evaluate them against the whispers of your innermost desires.

Only through such introspection can you begin to untangle the threads of external demands from the fabric of your intrinsic passions, and pave the way to a life that resonates with the essence of your true self.

As you embark upon this voyage toward authenticity, it becomes crucial to weave a net of supporters who not only recognize the beauty of your unique pattern but also encourage its growth.

In the pursuit of self-discovery, the companionship of others who delight in your individuality and bolster your resolve to follow your bliss can be both affirming and invigorating.

Cultivating relationships with those who applaud your differences and push you towards self-exploration adds vibrancy to your journey, enabling you to bloom amidst a garden of allies.

As you seek out and nurture these connections, whether within a community, through mentorship, or in laughter-filled conversations with friends, you create a safe harbor from which you can voyage confidently into the seas of your own destiny.

Let's explore some powerful steps to release yourself from conformity and expectations, and to create a life that honors your unique design.

Step 1: Set Boundaries with Unsupportive Individuals

Navigating the unique journey of life, we each bring our distinct symphony of traits, dreams, and quirks to the world's grand concert.

However, amidst this rich tapestry, it is imperative to recognize the individuals who, intentionally or not, fail to cherish our originality, pressing their own expectations upon our canvas.

These characters in our story can be anyone—a friend, a family member, or a colleague—whose well-meaning counsel often underscores their vision rather than our authentic selves.

Setting boundaries, though seemingly daunting, is an essential act of self-care, a courageous affirmation of our right to be ourselves.

Engage these individuals with transparency and kindness, expressing your gratitude for their concern while firmly shaping the narrative of your life's unfolding saga.

For instance, when a family member's critical lens on your choices clouds your inner clarity, gently assert your individuality and the significance of their support on your path.

Remember, the heart of setting boundaries lies in opening a channel for honest communication, sifting through expectations, and firmly rooting yourself in the soils of your unique being.

The sanctuary of a supportive circle—friends who encourage, family who uplift—cultivates an environment where our inner seeds of potential can germinate and bloom.

Nevertheless, not all companions traverse the path of our well-being with compassionate footprints.

Mastering the art of discernment is, therefore, vital; identifying those whose presence may wilt the spirit requires resilience and determination.

Should a friend's words continually cast shadows on the light of your goals, initiating a heartfelt dialogue reflects both the strength of your conviction and the depth of your self-respect.

Sometimes, the maintenance of boundaries may necessitate stepping away from relationships marinating in negativity.

Picture a workplace where you strive for excellence, yet a colleague perpetually drizzles your efforts with criticism; here, limiting engagement can be a powerful statement of intent.

Cultivating positive connections within the workplace then becomes a fertile ground for growth.

The essence of setting boundaries is never about confrontation; rather, it symbolizes a dynamic stand for one's well-being and the pursuit of an environment that vibrates with positivity.

By thoughtfully curating your social garden with those who value and uplift you, you empower yourself to unfold into the grandest version of who you are meant to be—a sovereign soul, magnificent in its unique journey.

Here are some additional steps:

Identify the unsupportive individuals in your life who consistently disrespect your boundaries or impose their expectations on you.

Reflect on the specific behaviors or comments from these individuals that make you feel uncomfortable or unappreciated.

Acknowledge that it is okay to prioritize your own well-being and set boundaries with those who do not support you.

Consider what type of boundaries you need to set with these unsupportive individuals in order to feel respected and valued.

Plan a time to have an honest and open conversation with the unsupportive individuals about your needs and boundaries.

Clearly communicate to them what behaviors or comments are unacceptable and why they are not supportive of you.

Be firm in expressing that you expect to be treated with respect and support in your choices and decisions.

Set consequences for when boundaries are not respected, such as limiting time with these individuals or seeking support from others.

Consistently enforce your boundaries, even if it means distancing yourself from unsupportive individuals when necessary.

Surround yourself with people who uplift and support you, and remind yourself that you deserve to be respected and valued.

Step 2: Practice Self-Compassion and Self-Care

Embracing self-compassion is similar to applying a soothing balm to the spirit, particularly as you endeavor to step away from the constraints of societal norms and expectations.

This journey of individuality often brings with it a silent pressure to measure up to a normative benchmark set by the masses.

In those moments when you notice yourself slipping into the throes of comparison or wrestling with the nagging notion that you're falling short of where you "should" be, pause and breathe.

Recognize that these self-imposed timelines and checkpoints are mirages on the unique path you tread.

Speak to yourself with the tender tone you would offer a dear friend – reaffirm your worth, celebrate your courage to defy conformity, and remember that your value is not contingent upon a societal yardstick.

This inner dialogue of kindness and understanding is a pillar of strength as you carve out your own place in the world.

Turning to the sacred practice of self-care, it's crucial to identify the things that serve as a wellspring of joy and restoration for you.

Perchance it's the gentle caress of water in a lingering bath or the intimate solace found between the pages of a gripping novel.

It might be the laughter shared in the company of a cherished companion. Attune yourself to these sources of comfort and make conscientious efforts to mesh them into the fabric of your daily life.

If the whisper of leaves and the embrace of the open sky are what call to your soul, then dedicate moments of your week to wander amidst nature's tapestry.

In the act of cherishing these instances, you're not indulging in frivolous luxury but rather honoring the essence of who you are.

You're not just a bystander in the progression of life; you're crafting a narrative steeped in self-love and attentiveness.

Let the cultivation of your well-being be your guiding compass, lighting the path toward inner peace and calmness.

Your life's journey is exclusively yours – navigate it with compassion in your heart and a steadfast commitment to nurturing your whole being.

Here are some additional steps:

Schedule regular self-care time:

Set aside time in your schedule for activities that bring you joy and relaxation, such as reading, going for a walk, or taking a hot bath.

Practice mindfulness and meditation:

Take time each day to practice mindfulness and meditation to cultivate self-compassion and reduce stress.

Seek therapy or counseling:

Consider seeking professional help if you are struggling with your mental health or need support in developing self-compassion.

Set boundaries:

Learn to say no to activities or commitments that drain your energy and prioritize activities that bring you joy and fulfillment.

Practice self-compassionate self-talk:

Be kind to yourself and practice positive self-talk to cultivate self compassion.

Prioritize sleep:

Ensure that you are getting enough rest and recharge your body and mind by prioritizing sleep.

Engage in physical activity:

Regular exercise can improve your mood, reduce stress, and boost your overall well-being.

Connect with others:

Seek out social support and connect with friends and loved ones who can provide encouragement and understanding.

Practice gratitude:

Take time each day to reflect on the things you are grateful for and cultivate a positive mindset.

Reflect on your progress:

Take time to reflect on your journey to self-compassion and self-care, and celebrate your progress and growth.

Step 3: Let Go of Societal Pressures and Judgments

In a world brimming with subliminal messages of what and how we ought to be, it becomes increasingly challenging to remain grounded to our authentic selves.

The societal lens often distorts our reflection, instilling a sense of inadequacy and evoking insecurities within us.

Recognizing these external pressures is the initial, transformative step toward reclaiming our individuality.

If you find that society's expectations of beauty or achievement weigh heavily upon you, pause and gently remind yourself that these imposed standards are fleeting and do not define your essence.

Embrace the vulnerability in self-acceptance, for when you start to cherish your unique attributes—the curve of your smile, the depth of your thoughts—you nullify the power of these outside pressures.

You offer a variety of qualities that are not up for societal assessment.

Remember, radiance shines brightest from within, and love for oneself is a love that resonates most profoundly.

Next time the mirror of society reflects an image that doesn't align with who you truly are, stand firm in your singular beauty, and celebrate the elements that distinguish you from the rest.

Many of us have felt the gnawing unease that accompanies societal benchmarks—the "proper" career trajectory, the relationship timeline etched out by a nonexistent hand.

When the noise of the world's expectations becomes too much, protect your peace by reminding yourself that life's symphony does not adhere to a universal tempo.

Each of us dances to a distinct rhythm, each of us crafts a narrative that is not meant to mimic another's.

Those moments when you find the courage to lean into what fuels your passion and happiness are the moments that truly measure success.

Dismiss the notion that worth is a commodity set against societal barometers.

Trust your instincts, lean into your skills, and craft a path that resonates with your deepest convictions.

And when it comes to the tapestry of human connections and personal choices, let the threads of sincerity weave the patterns that suit you best.

To move through life embracing your individuality is the epitome of freedom—to choose whom and how you love, to stand unapologetically for your values, and to forge an existence led by the drumbeat of your own heart is both empowering and liberating.

Remember, when you have the audacity to be unencumbered by societal dictates, you unfold the wings of personal liberation.

Here are some additional steps:

Acknowledge the societal pressures and judgments that you feel are affecting you.

Understand that these pressures and judgments are not a reflection of your worth or capabilities.

Take a step back and reflect on what truly matters to you and makes you happy.

Challenge and question the societal expectations and standards that are causing you stress or anxiety.

Surround yourself with supportive and understanding individuals who encourage and empower you to be yourself.

Practice self-compassion and remind yourself that it's okay not to fit into societal molds.

Embrace your individuality and uniqueness, and celebrate the things that make you different from others.

Set boundaries and limit your exposure to people or environments that fuel societal pressures and judgments.

Focus on personal growth and self-improvement based on your own values and aspirations, rather than external influences.

Reclaim your confidence and self-worth by letting go of the need to seek validation from societal standards and judgments.

Step 4: Surround Yourself with Positive and Uplifting Influences

Delving into the world of community groups can be a transformative experience and a cornerstone for personal development.

Imagine stepping into a room filled with individuals whose eyes sparkle with the same excitement for the cause that stirs your heart.

Be it through the pages of captivating novels in a book club, the shared breathlessness atop a beautiful outlook with your hiking peers, or the collective satisfaction of contributing to a cause in a volunteer group; such connections fortify our sense of purpose and belonging.

Imagine marching alongside fellow environmental enthusiasts in a conservation effort, each step echoing your commitment to Earth's well-being.

Their unwavering enthusiasm becomes a beacon that lights your path, reinforcing the notion that together, your aligned efforts can birth significant change.

By intertwining your journey with theirs, you not only expand your social horizons but also cement a fellowship dedicated to the greater good, a foundation that will support and inspire you to reach new heights in your personal quest for fulfillment and societal contribution.

Venturing beyond communal affiliations, establishing mentorship relationships stands as a mighty pillar in the construction of your aspirations.

The guidance of a seasoned mentor acts as a lighthouse in the often-turbulent sea of professional and personal growth.

Visualize having a mentor in the field of writing—someone who has woven their wisdom between the lines of their experiences.

Such a mentor helps chart your course, offering tailored advice that navigates you through industry intricacies, enhancing your skills, and opening doors to opportunities previously obscured.

Similarly, the cherished company of friends and family unfolds a tapestry of emotional support where every thread is woven with encouragement and affirmation.

Imagine a friend whose faith in you is as unwavering as the stars or a family member whose support for your passions is as nurturing as the sun; such relationships form the bedrock of your resilience and self-esteem.

By consciously choosing to be enveloped in this cocoon of positivity, your own unique colors shine brighter, and the wings of your dreams find the strength to soar.

Remember, in the revolution of positivity, the element of human connection is the most potent catalyst for transformation and joy.

Here are some additional steps:

Identify the negative influences in your life that may be holding you back from being true to yourself.

Make a conscious effort to distance yourself from these negative influences, whether it be toxic friendships, unsupportive family members, or negative media.

Seek out positive and uplifting individuals who support your growth and authenticity.

Connect with like-minded individuals who share similar values and goals.

Join supportive communities or groups that align with your interests and aspirations.

Engage in activities and hobbies that bring you joy, and surround yourself with people who share your passions.

Surround yourself with individuals who celebrate your uniqueness and encourage you to be true to yourself.

Seek out mentors or role models who inspire and uplift you, whether it be in person or through books, podcasts, or other forms of media.

Set boundaries with individuals who bring negativity into your life and prioritize spending time with those who bring out the best in you.

Continuously evaluate the influences in your life and make adjustments as necessary to ensure you are surrounded by positivity and uplifting energy.

Step 5: Embrace Your Independence and the Right to Choose Your Own Path

At the heart of embracing your independence is a deep-seated trust in yourself and your instincts. This is the compass that guides you through life's vast ocean of choices.

Consider the artist within who thrums at the sight of a blank canvas: if that passion for painting roars louder than the whispers of a conventional career, then to embrace your independence is to heed that call.

It requires the bravery to stride along the path of the heart where every stroke of the brush is a step towards personal fulfillment. Your life is your masterpiece, painted with decisions that serve your happiness above all else.

When you embrace your independence, you honor the most authentic parts of yourself, crafting a life that resonates with your deepest desires and dreams.

Choosing your own path is similar to keeping the windows of your soul open to the winds of every horizon.

If a wanderlust for the world's colors and cultures tugs at your spirit, yet you find yourself anchored by the weight of comfort zones, remember that stepping into independence is similar to unfolding the sails of adventure.

With every new venture comes a tapestry of experiences that enrich your life, infusing it with joy and vigor.

Realize that the mosaic of existence is replete with endless tiles waiting to be placed by your hand.

And as the architect of your journey, you have the liberty to sidestep the shadows cast by others' judgments or expectations.

Crafting a life that is unequivocally yours is the ultimate expression of independence, a declaration that the narrative of your life is for you to author, each chapter a testament to a spirit undimmed by the gaze of the world.

Here are some additional steps:

Reflect on your values and beliefs to understand what truly matters to you.

Take time to explore different options and possibilities for your future path.

Seek out advice and support from trusted friends, family, and mentors to gain insight and perspective.

Listen to your intuition and inner guidance when making important decisions.

Recognize that it's okay to stray from societal expectations and norms to follow your own unique path.

Embrace the idea that failure and setbacks are a natural part of the journey toward independence and self-discovery.

Take ownership of your choices and actions, knowing that they are a reflection of your independence and personal deeds.

Practice assertiveness and speak up for what you believe in, even if it goes against the grain.

Surround yourself with people who support and respect your independence, and distance yourself from those who try to control or limit your choices.

Celebrate and honor your individuality and the path you have chosen, knowing that it is a reflection of your personal freedom.

Ways to Shedding the "Shoulds" and Embracing Your True Self

Embracing authenticity:

Liberating yourself from societal pressures

Finding your true self:

Shedding expectations and embracing individuality.

Unleashing potential:

Releasing yourself from the constraints of conformity

Defying expectations:

Liberating yourself from societal norms.

Discovering freedom:

Letting go of society's "shoulds" and embracing true freedom.

Unmasking your true self:

Shedding societal expectations and embracing authenticity.

Empowerment through individuality:

Breaking free from the pressures of conformity

Authentic living:

Liberating yourself from society's expectations and embracing your true self

Accepting your unique self:

Shedding the "shoulds" and embracing personal freedom.

<u>**Chapter Summary**</u>

- Set boundaries with unsupportive individuals.
- Practice self-compassion and self-care.
- Let go of societal pressures and judgments.
- Surround yourself with positive and uplifting influences.
- Embrace your independence and the right to choose your own path.

<u>**FAQ**</u>

How can I effectively set boundaries with unsupportive individuals in my life?

Setting boundaries with unsupportive individuals involves having honest conversations about your needs and clearly communicating what is acceptable and what is not.

For example, if a family member constantly criticizes your choices, you can kindly let them know that you appreciate their concern, but ultimately, it's your life, and you need their support.

What are some practical ways to practice self-compassion and self-care as I break free from conformity?

Practical ways to practice self-compassion and self-care include setting aside time for activities that bring you joy, seeking therapy or counseling, or simply practicing mindfulness and meditation to cultivate self-compassion.

How can I consciously choose to let go of societal pressures and judgments?

Consciously choosing to let go of societal pressures and judgments involves recognizing these influences and reminding yourself that you are unique and worthy just as you are.

It's about actively challenging the negative thoughts and beliefs imposed by society.

How can I embrace my independence and the right to choose my own path in life?

Embracing your independence and the right to choose your own path in life involves recognizing that you have the power to make decisions that align with your true self.

This could mean pursuing a career that reflects your passions, choosing a lifestyle that feels authentic to you, or simply making choices that honor your individuality.

What are some examples of unsupportive individuals in my life that I should set boundaries with?

Examples of unsupportive individuals could be family members, friends, or colleagues who impose their expectations on you and do not support your uniqueness.

How can I prioritize self-care while still meeting my other responsibilities?

You can prioritize self-care by setting aside specific time for activities that bring you joy and by learning to say no to additional responsibilities that may overwhelm you.

What are the potential consequences of not releasing myself from conformity and expectations?

The potential consequences of not releasing yourself from conformity and expectations include feeling unfulfilled, living a life that does not align with your true self, and experiencing high levels of stress and anxiety from trying to meet others' expectations.

Can you provide more specific examples of societal pressures and judgments that I should consciously let go of?

Some specific examples of societal pressures and judgments could include beauty standards, career expectations, or societal norms around family and relationships.

Having shaken off the weight of expectations and conformity, it's time to infuse our days with purposeful delight. In the next chapter, we'll explore the pathway to bliss and discover practical ways to find joy and fulfillment in our daily lives.

The Pathway to Bliss

Infusing Your Day with Purposeful Delight

"**M**ay the God of hope fill you with all joy and peace as you trust in him, so that you may overflow with hope by the power of the Holy Spirit." - Romans 15:13 NIV

- Understand the importance of engaging in activities that bring you happiness and how it positively impacts your well-being.

- Define your personal definition of success and align your actions with your unique purpose.

- Set achievable goals aligned with your values to work toward a fulfilling life that is uniquely yours.

- Create a supportive and nurturing environment by surrounding yourself with uplifting and inspiring people.

- Practice gratitude and mindfulness to cultivate a mindset that fosters a deeper sense of joy and purpose.

Blissful Reflection:

Uncover the Life-Changing Words That Brought Joy to an Entire Community

Once upon a time, in a quaint village nestled among rolling hills and whispering streams, there lived a young girl who was yearning for happiness and fulfillment.

Her heart was weighed down by the mundane routines of daily life, and her spirit longed for a sense of purpose that seemed just out of reach.

Each morning, she awoke with a sigh, looking out over the thatched roofs and cobblestone paths, wondering where the magic of life had gone.

One day, she approached a kind-hearted woman named Sarah and poured her heart out, sharing her struggles and doubts.

Sarah's small cottage was a place of solace for many; her reputation as a wise elder of the village was well-known.

The walls, adorned with beautiful tapestries and herbs, seemed to absorb the young girl's tales of woe, and Sarah listened without interruption, her eyes reflecting a soul that had learned to find peace in the middle of life's storms.

Sarah listened intently, her warm smile radiating genuine empathy and understanding.

The young girl felt a sense of relief in her presence, as if she could lay down the burdens of her heart.

Sarah's smile seemed to tell her that it was okay to not have all the answers and that there was a serene wisdom to be found in the acceptance of life's mysteries.

As the young girl finished her tale, Sarah took her hand and led her to a peaceful spot overlooking the village.

It was a sacred space where the gentle breeze carried the fragrance of wildflowers, and one could see the entire village living its daily rhythm.

Sarah gestured toward the horizon, where the first light of dawn cast a soft glow, and began to speak.

With a tender expression, Sarah spoke of a powerful verse from Psalms 118:24 NKJV—

> "This is the day that the Lord has made; let us rejoice and be glad in it."

She emphasized the importance of finding joy in the gift of each day, even in the face of adversity. "We must choose to see the silver lining,"

Sarah said, guiding the young girl to perceive each sunrise as a canvas of potential and every sunset as a lesson learned.

Then, Sarah recalled the wisdom in Ecclesiastes 3:13 NKJV—

> "and also that every man should eat and drink and enjoy the good of all his labor—it *is* the gift of God."

She highlighted the divine intention for joy and purpose in daily life, encouraging the young girl to savor the simple pleasures and embrace the beauty of her journey.

"Happiness is not a distant destination," Sarah explained, "but a path we walk every day, noticing the fruits in our basket and the flowers at our feet."

As they sat in peaceful silence, Sarah began to share an anecdote about the delicate and awe-inspiring nature of spider webs, each one a unique design intricately woven by its creator.

She drew parallels between the delicate patterns of spider webs and the intricate details of our own lives, each thread serving a purpose, each space a room for growth, each intersection a choice.

She expressed gratitude for the thoughtful and loving design woven by God, reminding the young girl that every aspect of her life was a part of a grand tapestry, with beauty waiting to be recognized.

Quoting Philippians 4:4 NKJV—

"Rejoice in the Lord always; again, I will say, rejoice,"

Sarah encouraged the young girl to cultivate joy and purpose in her daily life, embracing her one-of-a-kind design with gratitude and delight. "Joy is not just a fleeting emotion,"

Sarah said softly, "but a steady undercurrent that sustains us through all seasons, a strength that matures from deep within."

Inspired by Sarah's comforting words, the young girl began to infuse her days with purpose. She spent time in nature, relishing the vibrant colors of the flowers and the gentle melody of the wind.

These simple acts recharged her spirit, opening her eyes to the world's beauty that she had long ignored.

She engaged in creative activities that brought her happiness, such as painting and singing—not to impress others, but as a sincere expression of her inner joy.

She redefined her personal definition of success, shifting her focus from external achievements to inner contentment.

She remembered the verse from Colossians 3:23 NKJV—

"And whatever you do, do it heartily, as to the Lord and not to men,"

With this in mind, she found fulfillment and purpose in serving the Lord with all her heart, recognizing the beauty in small acts of kindness and love.

She discovered that when she dedicated her talents and time to a cause greater than herself, her work gained an eternal significance, and her heart was filled with a profound sense of accomplishment.

From that day on, the village was abuzz with newfound vitality and joy.

Sarah's wisdom echoed through the pathways, empowering others to embrace their quirky individuality and acknowledge their unique purpose in the Creator's greater plan.

Each person, with their one-of-a-kind design, reveled in the joyful and purposeful journey orchestrated by the Divine Weaver.

The village danced with gratitude and delight, each person nurturing a heart brimming with joy.

And as they delighted in their own unique designs, they found solace and fulfillment, each day a precious gift to be treasured.

Simple acts of generosity and kindness became the norm, as the villagers understood that their happiness was inextricably linked to the happiness of others.

They fostered a community where everyone was seen, understood, and valued.

As the sun dipped below the horizon, casting its golden light upon the village, the residents gathered in a circle, holding hands with bright smiles illuminating their faces.

They felt a powerful sense of connection, as if their hearts beat in unison, pulsing with a unified sense of gratitude.

Together, they recited the words from Proverbs 17:22 NKJV—

"A merry heart does good, *like* medicine,
But a broken spirit dries the bones."

These words had become their guiding light, a reminder to cultivate joy and purpose in daily life, to engage in activities that brought happiness, and to practice gratitude and mindfulness in alignment with their values and greater spiritual awareness.

And so, the village was forever transformed, each soul embarking on a journey of self-discovery and inner bliss.

They celebrated each day as a precious gift, finding purpose in the simple moments.

Their shared joy became a powerful force, healing wounds of the past and knitting their community closer together.

And as their joy overflowed, it spread like ripples in a pond, touching the lives of others and inspiring them to embrace their own divine design.

The village thrived, a tapestry of love, happiness, and purpose, each person weaving their own vibrant thread into the rich fabric of life, united by the common desire to live with joyful and purposeful hearts.

Their laughter rose to the heavens, a chorus of lives well-lived.

And as the stars twinkled above, mirroring the light of their souls, it was clear that they had uncovered the true essence of a life well-lived—a life lived with joy.

Embarking on your transformational journey toward a life steeped in joy and purpose isn't merely an aspiration—it's a conscious decision made each day.

To elicit true delight and infuse intention into your existence, consider every action you take as a brushstroke on the canvas of your life, painting a picture that resonates with your deepest values and desires.

It's a process of intentional living where every decision is an opportunity to invite vibrancy and happiness into your world. Imagine waking up each morning with an eagerness to embrace activities that electrify your soul, to engage in work that feels more like a calling, and to cultivate relationships that uplift and inspire.

As you align your life with the essence of who you truly are, each step you take on this pathway becomes a dance between your inner and outer worlds, bringing into being the unique masterpiece that is your life.

In practice, kindling the flames of joy and purpose requires a personal inventory—a heartfelt exploration into the nooks and crannies of your passions and pleasures.

Reflect upon what stirs excitement within you, whether it's the warm laughter shared with family and friends, the tranquil solitude of immersing yourself in a cherished hobby, or the profound satisfaction of extending a helping hand to those in need.

With these nuggets of happiness identified, pledge to weave them into the fabric of your daily routine.

By consciously dedicating time to engage in these joy-sparking activities, you nourish your spirit and fan the embers of contentment. Simultaneously, dare to align your actions with your innermost values.

When your day-to-day life echoes the symphony of your true desires, you anchor yourself in authenticity.

Take stock of where you invest your energy and ensure it reflects your personal character.

As you do this, you'll discover your experiences become imbued with greater depth, contributing to a life brimming with fulfillment and a profound connection to the essence of you.

By taking these steps, you'll find that you naturally become more blissfully unique as you embrace your true self.

Step 1: Engage in Activities that Bring You Happiness

Embracing the activities that infuse your life with happiness isn't just about having fun; it's about glowing from the inside out.

Consider the painter whose brush dances across the canvas, where every stroke is a testament to the joy of creation.

When you clear space in your week for the simple act of painting, you're not just filling your surroundings with color; you're filling your soul with fulfillment.

In this dedicated corner of your world, clutter gives way to creativity, and time loses its urgency as you surrender to the flow of the present moment.

Such purposeful engagement in self-expression acts as a gateway to bliss, inviting you to explore the depths of your imagination while joyfully adrift in the sea of artistic endeavor.

Similarly, life's essence often sparkles most brightly in the company of loved ones. Their laughter and the warmth of shared memories have a unique way of lighting up life's journey.

Cherish these bonds by carving time out of your bustling life for those heart-to-heart dinners or blissful outings that weave the fabric of your relationships tighter.

In doing so, you're not just catching up; you're building a sanctuary of support, a community where happiness is shared and multiplied.

Such acts of love are a beacon of positivity in a world often riddled with solitude, for in giving joy through your presence, you, too, are bathed in its radiant glow.

Balance your life with these gatherings, and watch as your well-being blossoms in a garden of collective contentment.

Here are some additional steps:

Identify activities that bring you happiness.

Schedule regular time for these activities in your daily or weekly routine.

Set goals for these activities, whether it's learning a new song on the guitar or planting a beautiful garden.

Share these activities with friends or family to spread joy and create meaningful connections.

Practice mindfulness and be fully present in the moment while engaging in these activities.

Reflect on the positive impact these activities have on your mental and emotional well-being.

Seek out new activities or hobbies to explore and expand your sources of happiness.

Take time to appreciate and savor the feelings of joy and fulfillment that come from engaging in these activities.

Continuously prioritize and make time for these activities in your life to maintain a sense of happiness and contentment.

Step 2: Define Your Personal Definition of Success

Success, as subjective as it is, demands introspection to define. To some, it is manifested in the glint of achievement in a chosen career; for others, it blooms within the embrace of loved ones.

The equilibrium of work-life balance might define it for many, while personal growth and self-improvement sketch success for the rest.

This medley of meanings prompts the necessity to pause and delve into the essence of what truly resonates with you.

The journey to align your actions with your unique definition of success requires an honest conversation with yourself, setting the cornerstone for a life tailored to your fulfillment.

Envision your success not as a distant peak to conquer, but as a garden that flourishes with each step of your journey.

My perception weaves success into the fabric of both my personal and professional spheres, harmonizing them to reflect a life of satisfaction.

It's about igniting passion in my career in a way that echoes my core values, touching lives, and imprinting a positive mark.

Cultivating enduring bonds with family and friends serves as an anchor, reinforcing the belief that growth is not in isolation but in connection.

Success, therefore, is tranquil satisfaction in being true to oneself, in accomplishments big and small, and in the unquantifiable contentment that perforates through every life domain.

Grant yourself a license to redefine success on your terms, setting examples that resonate with your inner compass.

Picture a career that doesn't just fill a bank account, but also fills your heart with its contributions to the world – be that through art, service, or advocacy.

Imagine a seamless weave between dedication to your craft and devotion to your own well-being, alongside the joy of relationships.

Elevate the paradigm of success to include relentless pursuits of self-betterment, through learning, embracing novel experiences, and introspective reflection.

To walk this path, I commit to personal milestones that mirror my deepest values, apply deliberate efforts toward reaching them, and hold fast to the insight that success is a perpetual expedition, rich with discovery and genuine contentment.

Embrace this voyage, not merely as a traveler but as the surveyor of your journey, marking each achievement as a waypoint of joy and fulfillment in the map of your life.

Here are some additional steps:

Reflect on your values and priorities.

Consider what aspects of your life are most important to you.

Identify your long-term goals and aspirations.

Determine what accomplishments would make you feel successful.

Consider how you want to feel on a daily basis.

Think about the legacy you want to leave behind.

Evaluate what success looks like in different areas of your life.

Consider the impact you want to have on others.

Create a clear and detailed definition of success that aligns with your personal values and aspirations.

Use your definition of success as a guide for making decisions and setting goals in your life.

Step 3: Set Achievable Goals Aligned with Your Values

Understanding what brings you joy and how you define success marks the beginning of a transformative journey.

The goals you set henceforth play a pivotal role in manifesting the life you envision—one that resonates with your soul's calling.

Remember, these goals don't have to be monumental to be meaningful; the smallest of strides, when aligned with your true self, can propel you toward immense fulfillment.

Strive for goals that mirror the unique tapestry of your values and passions.

Perhaps it is learning a new skill that sets your heart ablaze or forging deeper connections with loved ones.

Maybe it's embarking on a path to improve your well-being or creating something that will leave a lasting imprint on the world.

Let these aspirations be your guiding stars, irrespective of the magnitude or timeline. What matters most is their likeness with the essence of who you are and their power to illuminate your journey toward an authentic and satisfying life.

Embrace the personal evolution that goal setting affords without succumbing to the pressures of external benchmarks.

This is not a race, nor is it a contest—it is your unique narrative unfolding one goal at a time.

Let go of societal metrics that often overshadow our true desires and lean into the independence of crafting a life that's in harmony with your deepest inclinations.

As you take this time for introspection, consider the milestones that will serve as signposts on your path, guiding you closer to your ideal existence.

With each goal achieved, you'll not only inch closer to the life you've dreamed of, but you'll also expand your capacity for joy and fulfillment.

The act of setting and pursuing goals in tune with your authentic self is an expression of self-love and an unwavering commitment to the life you are destined to lead.

Stand at the wheel of your destiny, chart your course with heartfelt goals, and let each step be a joyful dance toward a life of purpose and happiness.

Here are some additional steps:

Reflect on your values:

Take some time to identify and clarify what values are most important to you in life.

Prioritize your values:

Determine which values are the most significant to you and will guide your goal-setting process.

Assess your current situation:

Take stock of where you are in relation to your values and where you want to be in the future.

Set specific goals:

Based on your values, create specific and measurable goals that you want to achieve.

Break down your goals:

Divide your goals into smaller, more manageable steps that you can work toward.

Be realistic:

Ensure that your goals are achievable and within reach, taking into account your current resources and limitations.

Make a timeline:

Establish a timeline for when you want to achieve each of your goals, whether short-term or long-term.

Plan for obstacles:

Anticipate potential challenges and brainstorm strategies to overcome them in order to stay aligned with your values.

Monitor your progress:

Regularly track your progress toward your goals and adjust your actions as needed.

Celebrate your achievements:

When you reach your goals, take time to celebrate your accomplishments and recognize how they align with your values.

Step 4: Create a Supportive and Nurturing Environment

Embarking on the journey of each day with purposeful delight requires more than mere intention; it involves the construction of a supportive and nurturing environment that serves as the bedrock for our well-being.

Encircle yourself with individuals who exude positivity, those who are wellsprings of inspiration and motivators for the pursuit of your aspirations and dreams.

If you notice that some relationships consistently leave you feeling unfilled or zapped of energy, it's prudent to reflect on those connections and realign them to suit your quest for growth.

Remember, the people in our lives are similar to the soil in which we plant ourselves - they can either enrich our growth or stunt it.

By consciously nurturing relationships that are supportive and sustaining, you'll find your environment becomes a fertile ground where your potential can flourish and where every day is tinted with the hue of fulfillment and joy.

Nurturing your environment extends beyond the emotional and social spheres into the physical realms where you spend your time. One's abode should be a sanctuary of tranquility and inspiration.

Try introducing elements that engage your senses in a warm embrace - soft lighting that winks at you with warmth, blankets that offer comfort like a friend's embrace, and fragrances such as lavender or eucalyptus that breeze through the air, whispering calm into the chaos of the day.

Like a canvas awaiting the artist's touch, infuse your living spaces with items that resonate with your essence - perhaps it's the motivational quotes that serve as reminders of strength, photographs echoing laughter from days past, or art that stirs your soul to dance.

Similarly, transform your workspaces with life-giving plants, breathing freshness into your tasks, décor that speaks of aspirations, and melodies that set a tempo for productivity.

Every corner of your environment should be an altar upon which you lay offerings of creativity and gratefulness, a sacred space where every element conspires to cheer you on your path to purpose and passion.

Here are some additional steps:

Identify the people in your life who bring positivity, support, and encouragement, and make time to connect with them regularly.

Limit the time spent with individuals who bring negativity or drain your energy, and seek out relationships that bring joy and inspiration.

Establish clear boundaries with toxic environments or toxic people, and prioritize relationships that nurture and uplift you.

Create a physical space at home or in your workplace that promotes a sense of calm and positivity, whether through calming colors, inspiring artwork, or meaningful objects.

Designate a specific area in your home or office for activities that bring you joy and relaxation, such as reading, meditating, or practicing a hobby.

Incorporate elements of nature into your environment, such as plants, natural light, or soothing sounds, to create a sense of tranquility.

Practice regular decluttering and organization to create a clean and harmonious space, free from distractions and stressors.

Set aside time for self-care activities that promote your physical, mental, and emotional well-being, such as exercise, mindfulness practices, or creative expression.

Seek out opportunities to engage with a supportive community, whether through joining a club, attending events, or participating in group activities.

Continuously evaluate and adjust your environment and relationships to ensure they align with your values, goals, and overall sense of well-being.

Step 5: Practice Gratitude and Mindfulness

The simple act of expressing gratitude is a beacon of light in the daily grind, capable of transmuting the ordinary into the extraordinary.

In the gentle quietude of morning's first light or in the reflective silence of the day's end, pause to pen down the things that spark joy in your heart.

A simple list of grateful reflections—from the comfort of a cozy home to the enlivening presence of friends and family—can be a transformative ritual.

This practice becomes a magnet for positivity, drawing in the kind of abundant thinking that shapes a more optimistic outlook on life.

It's a way of acknowledging life's blessings, and by doing so, we begin to see that our lives are richer than we thought, flowing with gifts that merit our recognition and heartfelt thanks.

Mindfulness, too, stands as a powerful ally in our quest for daily delight, teaching us to inhabit the here and now with grace.

This meditative art can be woven into the tapestry of our lives seamlessly, requiring nothing more than a willingness to be still, to focus on the coming and going of our breath, or to engage wholly in the task at hand.

By anchoring ourselves in the present, we are gifted with the ability to relish the full spectrum of life's experiences, uncovering joy in the details that might have otherwise slipped by undetected.

The marriage of gratitude and mindfulness forms an altering, that transforms the mundane, infusing our routine with a deep wellspring of purposeful joy.

Our lives are but a canvas, and with gratitude and mindfulness as our brushes, we paint each day with vibrant strokes of fulfillment and bliss, creating a masterpiece that resonates with the soul's longing for happiness and meaning.

Our journey is ours to shape; with a heart full of thanks and a mind attuned to the present, we find that the path toward genuine contentment and success is illuminated by the simple, profound practices we choose to cultivate.

<u>Here are some additional steps:</u>

Set aside dedicated time each day to practice gratitude and mindfulness, whether it's in the morning, during a lunch break, or before bed.

Find a quiet and comfortable space where you can be alone and undisturbed for a few minutes.

Take a few deep breaths to center yourself and focus on the present moment.

Begin by thinking about the things you are grateful for in your life, such as your health, relationships, or personal achievements.

Write down or mentally acknowledge these things, and try to connect with the positive emotions they bring.

Shift your focus to the present moment, using your senses to ground yourself in the here and now.

Pay attention to the sights, sounds, smells, and physical sensations around you, without judgment or attachment.

If your mind wanders, gently bring it back to the present moment without getting frustrated with yourself.

Practice gratitude and mindfulness throughout your day, whether it's during routine activities or during moments of stress or difficulty.

Over time, these practices will become a natural part of your daily life, leading to greater happiness, resilience, and a deeper sense of purpose.

Ways to Embrace the Present Moment:

Find a quiet and comfortable space where you can sit or stand without distractions.

Take a few deep breaths to ground yourself and center your mind.

Close your eyes and begin to focus on the sensations of your breath as it moves in and out of your body.

As you continue to breathe, bring your awareness to the physical sensations in your body, noting any areas of tension or ease.

Begin to expand your awareness of the environment around you, noticing the sights, sounds, and smells without judgment or attachment.

Allow yourself to fully immerse in the present moment, letting go of any worries or anxieties about the past or future.

Take note of the things you are grateful for in this moment, whether it's the warmth of the sun on your skin or the sound of birds singing in the distance.

Practice expressing gratitude for these things, either silently in your mind or by speaking them out loud.

Take a moment to reflect on how these mindful and grateful moments have made you feel, and acknowledge any positive emotions that arise.

When you are ready, slowly open your eyes and return to the present moment, carrying this sense of mindfulness and gratitude with you throughout your day.

Chapter Summary

- Engage in activities that bring you happiness.

- Define your personal definition of success.

- Set achievable goals aligned with your values.

- Create a supportive and nurturing environment.

- Practice gratitude and mindfulness.

FAQ

How can I engage in activities that bring me happiness?

You can engage in activities that bring you happiness by making time for things that you enjoy and that bring you joy.

This could include activities like painting, gardening, playing music, spending time with loved ones, or simply enjoying a quiet moment alone with a good book.

What are some examples of defining my personal definition of success?

Examples of defining your personal definition of success could include having a fulfilling career, nurturing strong relationships, achieving a healthy work-life balance, or pursuing personal growth and self-improvement.

How do I set achievable goals aligned with my values?

You can set achievable goals aligned with your values by reflecting on what brings you joy and how you define success, and then setting goals that reflect those desires and values.

For example, if you value meaningful relationships, a goal could be to reach out to a friend or family member each week to maintain and nurture those connections.

What can I do to create a supportive and nurturing environment?

You can create a supportive and nurturing environment by surrounding yourself with people who uplift and inspire you, and who encourage you to pursue your dreams and passions.

Additionally, you can create physical spaces that promote a sense of peace and positivity, such as your home, office, or a special corner dedicated to your personal growth and well-being.

How can I practice gratitude and mindfulness in my daily life?

You can practice gratitude and mindfulness in your daily life by taking time each day to reflect on the things you are grateful for, and by incorporating practices like a daily gratitude journal or taking a few minutes each morning for meditation to help you be present in the moment and appreciate the richness of each experience and interaction.

Why is it important to engage in activities that bring me happiness?

Engaging in activities that bring you happiness is important because it nurtures your soul and infuses your days with positivity.

By prioritizing activities that bring you joy, you are prioritizing your own well-being and setting the stage for a more joyful, purposeful life.

Why should I define my personal definition of success?

Defining your personal definition of success is important because it helps you understand what brings fulfillment and meaning to your life.

By understanding your own unique definition of success, you can align your actions with that definition and live a purposeful life that is uniquely yours.

What is the benefit of practicing gratitude and mindfulness?

Practicing gratitude and mindfulness has the benefit of evolving a mindset that connects you to the present moment and promotes a deeper sense of joy and purpose.

It allows you to appreciate the richness of each experience and interaction, and creates a deeper connection to the world around you.

How can I align my daily actions with my definition of success?

You can align your daily actions with your definition of success by setting achievable goals that reflect your desires and values.

For example, if your personal definition of success involves pursuing creative endeavors, you can set aside time each day to work on your art, writing, or whatever form of creativity brings you fulfillment.

Now that we've explored the pathway to bliss, let's delve deeper into finding inner peace through spiritual awareness in the next chapter. It's time to tap into our spiritual GPS and discover how to navigate our lives with a greater sense of purpose and tranquility.

Spiritual GPS

FINDING INNER PEACE THROUGH SPIRITUAL AWARENESS

"The heavens declare the glory of God; the skies proclaim the work of his hands." - Psalm 19:1 (NIV)

- Establish a regular meditation and reflection practice to deepen your spiritual awareness.

- Find inner peace and spiritual connection by immersing yourself in nature or sacred spaces.

- Explore and understand different spiritual practices and beliefs to find what resonates with you.

- Seek knowledge and wisdom from spiritual texts to guide you on your spiritual journey.

- Connect with like-minded individuals in spiritual communities for support and encouragement.

Blissful Reflection:

Witness the Astonishing Spiritual Awakening of a Village Through the Inspiration of Cloud Formations

In the small, tranquil village nestled amongst verdant hills, there lived a kind-hearted woman named Abigail, who had eyes as clear and blue as the midday sky.

Abigail was not merely a fixture of the village's charm, but a beacon of wisdom, emanating a deep spiritual awareness that seemed to ripple through the very air.

Her connection with the beauty of the natural world was not one of mere appreciation, but a profound communion that spoke to the souls of those around her.

As fulfilling as her solitary reflections were, Abigail felt a calling to share this sense of wonder with her neighbors, knowing that true beauty grows exponentially when witnessed through multiple pairs of eyes.

One evening, as the sun's rays retreated and a cool serenity descended upon the village, Abigail gathered the villagers beneath the vast canvas of the open sky.

Together, they stood, enveloped by the encroaching dusk, to witness the breathtaking display of clouds, a fleeting tapestry of gold and amber.

It was here, under this celestial gallery, that Abigail began to weave her story, speaking not just with words, but with the reflective silence in between.

She brought to their minds Psalm 46:10 NKJV—

"Be still, and know that I *am* God;
I will be exalted among the nations,
I will be exalted in the earth!"

Emphasizing that within the quietude of reflection lies the possibility of a profound spiritual connection, a sacred space where one might commune with the divine and glean insights far beyond the reaches of spoken language.

She recounted the clouds, those ever-changing messengers of the sky, each pattern unique and transient, yet part of an infinite masterpiece. Abigail described how these cloud formations inspired awe and wonder, mirroring our own short-lived lives.

Drawing from James 4:8 NKJV—

"Draw near to God and He will draw
near to you. Cleanse *your* hands, *you* sinners; and puri-
fy *your* hearts, *you* double-minded."

she encouraged the villagers to seek their own spiritual closeness by embracing the symphony of nature that played endlessly around them.

The simple act of bearing witness to such unassuming grandeur, she proposed, was a pathway to feeling the divine pulse within the universe and within themselves.

Abigail's anecdotes were rich with the boundless creativity and artistry of the skies above.

She spoke with passionate gratitude for the Creator's love, which could be seen in the meticulous detail and imagination displayed across the cloudscape.

With Philippians 4:8 NKJV in her heart —

"Finally, brethren, whatever things are true, whatever things *are* noble, whatever things *are* just, whatever things *are* pure, whatever things *are* lovely, whatever
things *are* of good report, if *there is* any virtue and if *there
is* anything praiseworthy—meditate on these things."

she encouraged the villagers to seek reflection in this splendor.

The quiet majesty of cloud formations, she proposed, was a reminder that their own lives mirrored the Creator's attention to detail and inherent love.

The villagers came to embrace the fragile beauty of the skies, allowing the shifting dance of the clouds to deepen their spiritual awareness.

They found solace in the transient artistry of the heavens, regarding each moment as precious and each pattern as a personal gift bestowed upon them.

This shared experience wove a new thread throughout the village, stitching together the hearts of the people with the spiritual essence that was the source of their newfound inspiration.

With the village pulsing with a new spiritual harmony, the concept of interconnectedness flourished, as they learned to cherish their unique individuality within the Creator's grand design.

Gratitude for life's simple pleasures unfolded within them, and each villager began to recognize the quirks and idiosyncrasies that collectively contributed to the beautifully diverse tapestry of their community.

Inspired by Abigail's wisdom, everyone started to acknowledge the value of their singular contributions to the intertwined narrative of their lives.

Over time, contentment blossomed from the fertile soil of spiritual connectedness. Each villager honored their own unique mark in the universe, just as they honored the impermanent art displayed in the sky day after day.

In this acknowledgment, they discovered an unshakeable sense of joy, their spirits lifted by the conscious embrace of their own distinct paths and the indescribable wonder of the world around them.

The transformation within the village was undeniable.

The once-hushed whispers of day-to-day existence grew into a vibrant chorus of contentment and spiritual awareness.

The ritual of sky watching, initiated by Abigail's insight, became a communal practice, inviting each person to reflect upon the intimate link between the Creator's canvas and the countless ways in which their lives were woven into its expansive magnificence.

Abigail had sown the seeds of profound wisdom within the hearts of the villagers.

Through her gentle guidance, they had learned to stride alongside life's simple moments, finding delight and purpose within everyday wonders.

The villagers embraced the practice of drawing near to the Creator, trusting in the guidance they found in the unity and love reflected above them.

This trust did not go unreturned, for they realized that within each cloud's silver lining was an assurance of enduring companionship and guidance from a source far greater than themselves.

This message, rich with spiritual depth and contemplation, grew roots deep within the communal spirit of the village.

Learning to take heart in the Lord and let go of their worldly anxieties, the villagers found a peace that surpassed all their prior understanding.

It became their mantle, woven from the threads of serenity, simplicity, and a love that danced with the soft whispers of passing clouds.

The village, once a sanctuary of stillness, blossomed into a realm of warmth, joy, and profound spiritual connectedness.

In Abigail's tale, they had found an eternal font of solace, each individual discovering within themselves and the beauty of nature the pulse of the Creator's boundless love.

Guided by her spiritual wisdom, the villagers had each learned how to navigate life's journey, finding contentment in the masterpiece painted across the sky and in the understanding of their own intrinsic worth, with hearts ever aligned in the dance of clouds.

In our quest for a richer spiritual existence, it's essential to cultivate openness, allowing ourselves to be conduits for the infinite energy and wisdom that permeate the cosmos.

Engaging in introspective practices like meditation, prayer, and mindfulness can act as gateways to this profound connection.

By dedicating moments each day to quiet reflection, we provide ourselves with the opportunity to sync with the resonant frequency of the universe.

This harmonization not only calibrates our inner being to a state of peace and clarity but also ignites a sense of purpose and infuses our lives with meaning.

As you journey inward, remember that the universe speaks in the language of stillness, and within that silence, you'll discover the vibrant echoes of your own soul, gently guiding you toward enlightenment.

Embracing spiritual awareness is not just a solitary journey; it thrives in the warm company of others who share your yearning for universal connection.

Actively seek out communities, whether they are local groups, workshops, or digital havens, where spiritual dialogues flourish, and mutual growth is celebrated.

Immersing yourself in these supportive environments can exponentially magnify your spiritual experiences, providing a collective strength that uplifts each individual.

In doing so, you'll find a tribe where every story shared illuminates another piece of the grand cosmic puzzle.

As you venture deeper into the arms of spiritual enlightenment, let go of stubborn grips on desired outcomes.

Acknowledge the ebb and flow of life as part of a grander design, embracing surrender and trust as your vessels on this cruise across the ocean of existence.

With this acceptance comes the serenity of knowing that in the vast web of life, every twist, every turn, is a dance choreographed by the universe itself.

By cultivating these steps, you can create a sense of acceptance, gratitude, and compassion for yourself and others; you can find greater peace within and a sense of harmony with the world around you.

Step 1: Dedicate Time for Meditation and Reflection

Meditation and reflection are gateways to a world much larger than the physical spaces we inhabit.

When you allow yourself the grace to sit in silence, to gently push away the noisy demands of daily life, you open the door to profound spiritual depth.

This sacred practice tunes your senses to the subtle melodies of the universe, inviting you into a dance with the infinite.

As you clear your mind and center your thoughts on the rhythm of your breath, you are not merely pausing—you are listening, aligning, and harmonizing with the cosmos.

It is in these moments of stillness that the chatter of the external world falls away, and a deeper sense of awareness emerges.

This mindfulness is the fertile soil in which the seeds of spiritual growth robustly take root and flourish.

Begin this transformative journey with a compassionate invitation to your spirit: to seek, to explore, and to expand beyond the known.

Embarking on this path can be as simple as dedicating 10 minutes of your day to stillness and introspective serenity.

Choose a tranquil spot—a nurturing cocoon—where you can retreat from the commotion of routine.

Let your eyes softly close like the delicate petals of a flower at dusk, trusting the darkness to guard your peace. Inhale deeply, and as you exhale, envision casting off the weight of accumulated worries, allowing them to dissolve into the quiet around you.

As you focus on the ebb and flow of your breath, you'll discover it to be a timeless guide, steering you toward inner clarity and calm.

With each day and each practice, as your comfort with this intimate ritual grows, you too can grow—not only in the duration of your meditation sessions but also in the profound understanding of your place within the tapestry of existence.

Remember, this journey is yours to unfold with each breath, a step closer to the luminous essence of your being.

Here are some additional steps:

Find a quiet and comfortable space where you can sit undisturbed for meditation and reflection.

Set aside a specific time each day to dedicate to this practice, whether it's in the morning before starting your day or in the evening before bed.

Set a timer for a specific length of time, such as 10-20 minutes, to ensure you dedicate enough time for the practice without feeling rushed.

Sit down in a comfortable position, close your eyes, and focus on your breath.

Take deep, slow breaths to relax your body and mind.

Clear your mind of any distractions or thoughts and allow yourself to enter a state of peaceful stillness.

Focus on positive thoughts, affirmations, or a specific intention for your meditation and reflection.

Use visualization techniques to help you connect with your inner self.

Allow yourself to feel any emotions that arise during the practice and acknowledge them without judgment.

After the designated time, slowly open your eyes, take a few deep breaths, and gently return to the present moment.

Take a moment to reflect on your experience and any insights or revelations that may have come up during your meditation and reflection. This will help you integrate the practice into your daily life and continue to grow spiritually.

Step 2: Immerse Yourself in Nature or Sacred Spaces

There's something truly magical about being surrounded by the lush embrace of nature.

Wander down the winding path of a forest, where each step is an invitation to connect with the earth's harmonious symphony.

Breathe in deeply, and fill your lungs with the crisp scent of pine trees; let your ears tune into the cheerful serenade of birds, nature's original composers.

With each step, allow the world beneath your feet to anchor you into the present moment, binding your spirit to the intricate web of life that thrives in these green havens.

The forest offers not just a walk, but a journey of reconnection — to the wildness outside and the tranquility within.

Embrace this chance to be present, to observe the grandeur of nature's artistry, and to bask in the profound serenity that only the natural world can bestow.

Seeking out sacred spaces carries with it a promise of deep spiritual enrichment - they are epicenters of contemplation and awe, designed to elevate the soul.

Whether it is the echoing hush of a grand cathedral, the resplendent calm of a temple aglow with candles, or the unsung tranquility of a shrine secreted among mountain mists, each sacred site weaves a silent narrative of devotion and history that reverberates through time.

Embark on a pilgrimage to these revered havens, be it physically or through the contemplative journey of the mind.

Stand amidst their sanctity and let the weight of their legacy touch you; stand humbled by their beauty, and feel a communion with the countless hearts that have sought solace in their presence.

In the stillness that infuses these places, may you discover the reverberating echoes of your own inner sanctum, and carry with you the profound peace that such spaces so generously offer.

In every corner of the world, whether in the heart of a forest or the soul of a city, the doorways to nature's bounty and sanctified retreats lie open, awaiting your step through the threshold.

Even among the urban sprawl, pockets of peace — a park bench under a canopy of trees, a quiet garden where flowers nod in the breeze — invite you to claim moments of reflection.

The secret lies in embracing every opportunity to pause the relentless march of time, to breathe deeply the essence of the present, and to open your heart to the beauty and stillness that exists all around.

And in these moments spent in nature, or in sacred spaces, you will find not just relief but a profound reconnection, a coming home to the serenity and splendor that is ever-present, ever-waiting, just beneath the surface of our everyday lives.

Here are some additional steps:

Find a location:

Research and choose a natural setting or sacred space that resonates with you, whether it's a local park, a nearby mountain trail, or a place of worship.

Disconnect from technology:

Turn off your phone and any other distractions to fully immerse yourself in the experience of nature or the sacred space.

Practice mindfulness:

Take the time to be fully present in the moment, paying attention to the sights, sounds, and sensations around you.

Engage your senses:

Use all of your senses to fully experience the environment, whether it's feeling the sun on your skin, listening to the sounds of nature, or taking in the scents of flowers or incense.

Meditate or pray:

Take the opportunity to quiet your mind and connect with your inner self through meditation, prayer, or reflection.

Connect with others:

If you are in a natural setting, consider sharing the experience with friends or family members. If you are in a sacred space, consider participating in a group activity or ceremony.

Reflect on your experiences:

After your time in nature or sacred space, take some time to reflect on the emotions and insights that arose during your experience.

Express gratitude:

Take a moment to express gratitude for the beauty and wisdom that nature or the sacred space has provided.

Capture memories:

Consider taking photos, writing in a journal, or creating art to help preserve the memories and insights from your experience.

Integrate the experience into your daily life:

Find ways to carry the sense of peace and connection you experienced in nature or a sacred space into your everyday routines and interactions.

Step 3: Explore Different Spiritual Practices and Beliefs

Meditation stands as a beacon of tranquility in the bustling world we inhabit.

It is a spiritual bridge that connects us not only to the profound depths of our inner selves but also to the vast cosmos that engulfs us.

Delving into this practice, you may find that mindfulness meditation grounds you in the present, teaching you to embrace each moment with a gratifying breath of consciousness.

Loving-kindness meditation, on the other hand, expands the heart's capacity for compassion, radiating goodwill beyond the confines of the self.

And then there's transcendental meditation, which offers a passage to a state of restful awareness where the chatter of the mind dissolves into a symphony of silence.

Experiment with these forms, for each, holds a unique key to unlocking the doors to self-awareness and inner peace.

Let meditation be your sanctuary where the divine whispers and your soul listens.

As you tread gently upon this earth, the ancient wisdom of interconnectedness beckons you to perceive the world through a sacred lens.

This spiritual tapestry, woven into the essence of many indigenous cultures, unveils a universe where every creature, every plant, and every element is a strand in an inseparable web of life.

To explore this belief is to awaken to the profound responsibility we hold toward our planet and its numerous expressions of life.

This revelation kindles a passionate aspiration to live in rhythm with nature, nurturing a bond with the living earth that is at once nourishing and awe-inspiring.

Allow the spirit of interconnectedness to instill your actions and thoughts, so you may walk in beauty and balance upon this earth.

Embrace the holistic allure of yoga as a journey that transcends mere physical discipline and becomes a sacred dance of vitality and stillness.

As you flow through the postures, the pranayama breath work, and the meditative stillness at yoga's core, you touch a profound unity of body, mind, and spirit.

Whether it's the gentle foundation of Hatha yoga, the dynamic sequences of Vinyasa, or the transformative energy of Kundalini, each style offers a path that can lead to greater physical well-being and spiritual blossoming.

Welcome yoga into your life as a cherished companion on your quest for harmony and self-realization.

Embarking on this spiritual exploration, consider participating in workshops, listening to lectures, and absorbing the insights from books about diverse spiritual practices.

As you journey through the countless landscapes of spirituality, remain open and receptive to the lessons each tradition offers.

The wisdom of different cultures and belief systems is a treasure trove waiting to enrich your worldview, and, ultimately, to guide you to the truth that resonates with the core of your being.

May you find joy in this exploration and feel empowered to weave your unique tapestry of spiritual understanding.

Here are some additional steps:

Research and educate yourself about different spiritual practices and beliefs.

Reflect on your own beliefs and values.

Consider what aspects of spirituality are important to you.

Seek out books, articles, and videos about various spiritual practices and beliefs.

Connect with individuals practicing different spiritual traditions and ask about their experiences and insights.

Attend workshops, seminars, or events focused on different spiritual practices and beliefs.

Visit places of worship, sacred sites, or spiritual communities to gain a firsthand experience of different traditions.

Engage in meditation, prayer, or other contemplative practices from different spiritual traditions.

Keep an open mind and heart as you explore different spiritual practices and beliefs.

Integrate aspects of different spiritual traditions into your own spiritual practice if you feel called to do so.

Step 4: Seek Knowledge and Understanding from Spiritual Texts

Seeking knowledge and understanding from spiritual texts is like turning the pages of a vast treasure map, where the X marks the spot of inner wealth and peace.

These sacred writings have a divine way of whispering truths into the complexities of our lives, truths that have been reflected upon by countless souls before us.

Each word or verse can strike like a chord of harmony, resonating within the deepest facets of our being, inspiring us to navigate life's turbulent seas with an unwavering compass of hope and inner calm.

As you meander through the wisdom-laden paths these texts carve out; you may discover nuggets of enlightenment that help make sense of the enigma that is existence.

They beckon you to a quieter place within, where you'll find the serenity that braces your spirit against the storms of the outer world.

Let these words be your anchor and your sail, guiding you towards shores of tranquility and understanding.

As you embark on this rich journey, remember that the spiritual texts which align with your core beliefs and values will serve as the most potent catalysts for transformation.

Their teachings, when woven into the fabric of your daily life, are similar to threads of a divine tapestry; each thread strengthens your connection to the essence of who you are and the universe you are a part of.

This harmonious blend of ancient wisdom and personal experience paves the way for profound empathy and mindfulness.

Imagine starting each day with a passage that ignites your soul, or ending each evening with a reflection that soothes it—such rituals ground your thoughts and elevate your spirit.

As you absorb the essence of these words, you'll find that they don't just reside in the pages you turn but live in the choices you make, the patience you practice, and the love you share.

Let your quest for spiritual knowledge be a light that not only illuminates your path but also brightens the world around you.

With an open heart and mind, invite the wisdom of these spiritual texts to journey with you, and immerse yourself in the profound joy that comes from growing ever closer to the sacred dance of life.

<u>**Here are some additional steps:**</u>

Identify spiritual texts that resonate with your beliefs and values.

Set aside dedicated time for reading and studying these spiritual texts, allowing yourself to fully immerse in their wisdom and teachings.

Reflect on the messages and lessons within the texts, considering how they apply to your own life and spiritual journey.

Seek out additional resources, such as commentaries or study guides, to gain deeper insight and understanding into the spiritual texts.

Engage in discussions with others who are also interested in the same spiritual texts, sharing and exchanging perspectives and interpretations.

Practice mindfulness and meditation, using teachings from spiritual texts to guide your spiritual practice and self-reflection.

Keep an open mind and be willing to challenge your existing beliefs and perspectives, allowing the spiritual texts to expand and deepen your understanding.

Apply the principles and teachings from the spiritual texts into your daily life, embodying their wisdom and values in your actions and interactions with others.

Seek guidance from spiritual leaders, mentors, or practitioners who have a deep understanding, and can offer further insight and guidance.

Continuously seek knowledge and understanding from spiritual texts, recognizing that the journey toward enlightenment is an ongoing and ever-evolving process.

Step 5: Connect with Like-Minded Individuals in Spiritual Communities

The quest for meaning and connection drives many of us to find our tribe, those who resonate with the vibrations of our own hearts and souls.

Within spiritual communities, the sense of belonging and understanding that emerges when connecting with like-minded individuals is both powerful and profound.

Consider the tranquility that can be found in a meditation group, where each individual is on a personal quest for inner peace and self-discovery.

Such a sanctuary is a fertile ground for sharing experiences that are often transformative, providing a collective strength that positively supports each member's spiritual growth.

It is in these gatherings that hearts speak without words, where silent understanding weaves a tapestry of shared human experience, empowering one another to journey deeper into the realms of the spirit and mind.

Similarly, the practice of yoga connects us on multiple planes, inviting a communal exploration of mindfulness and bodily harmony.

Those who roll out their mats alongside us are more than just fellow practitioners; they are companions on a path toward greater awareness and unity with the divine essence of life.

The mutual energy in a yoga class can transcend the physical space, offering encouragement and inspiration that seep into daily life, bolstering our commitment to our spiritual practice.

And for those who yearn for a more immersive experience, spiritual retreats can be a beacon of light, summoning souls from all walks of life to delve into the shared pursuit of enlightenment.

In such retreats, the potency of collective intention in conversations and participatory practices forges iron-clad bonds and friendships that extend far beyond the realms of the retreat itself.

Remember, as you journey through these enlightening experiences, to savor each step, to remain open to the mysteries of the universe, and to relish the inner peace that comes with true spiritual connection.

Embrace the literature of bygone sages, the wisdom that has traversed through time, and let knowledge be both your compass and companion on this promising voyage of the soul.

Here are some additional steps:

Engage in meditation and mindfulness practices to quiet the mind and open yourself to spiritual insights.

Spend time in nature, connecting with the natural world to feel a deeper connection to the universe.

Seek out spiritual communities and connect with like-minded individuals who can support and guide you on your spiritual journey.

Practice gratitude and appreciation for the beauty and wonder of the universe, allowing yourself to feel a sense of awe and reverence for existence.

Engage in acts of service and compassion to connect with the interconnectedness of all living beings.

Explore different spiritual traditions and practices to gain a broader understanding of the diverse ways people connect with the divine.

Reflect on your life's purpose and how you can align your actions with your spiritual values and beliefs.

Seek out spiritual mentors or teachers who can offer guidance and support in deepening your connection to the universe.

Engage in regular spiritual practices such as prayer, ritual, or ceremony to foster a sense of connection to higher spiritual awareness.

<u>Ways to Discovering Your Spiritual Compass:</u>

Find a natural or sacred space to explore, such as a garden, forest, or mountain.

Take the time to fully immerse yourself in the surroundings, noticing the sights, sounds, and smells of nature.

Sit in quiet meditation or reflection, allowing yourself to feel connected to the energy and spirit of the natural world.

Practice deep breathing exercises to center yourself and quiet the mind.

Reflect on your own spiritual beliefs and values, seeking to find a sense of peace and alignment with your inner self.

Consider the role of spirituality in your life and how it contributes to your overall well-being.

Journal about your experiences and insights, documenting any feelings of inner peace or spiritual awareness that arise.

Engage in spiritual practices such as prayer, meditation, or mindfulness to further deepen your connection to your inner self.

Seek out opportunities for spiritual growth and learning, such as reading books or attending workshops on the subject.

Commit to regularly engaging in spiritual practices and seeking out moments of inner peace through nature and self-reflection.

Chapter Summary

- Dedicate time for meditation and reflection to deepen your connection with your inner self and achieve mindfulness.

- Immerse yourself in nature or sacred spaces to evoke a sense of peace and spiritual connection.

- Explore different spiritual practices and beliefs to find what resonates with you the most.

- Seek knowledge and understanding from spiritual texts to guide you on your spiritual journey.

- Connect with like-minded individuals in spiritual communities to find support and encouragement and form meaningful connections.

FAQ

How can I incorporate meditation into my daily routine to deepen my connection to the universe and experience a higher spiritual awareness?

You can start by setting aside a specific time each day for meditation, such as early in the morning or before bed.

Find a quiet and comfortable space, close your eyes, and focus on your breath. As you become more comfortable with the practice, you can gradually increase the duration of your meditation sessions.

What are some examples of sacred spaces I can visit to deepen my spiritual connection?

You can consider visiting natural places such as parks, mountains, or beaches, as well as man-made sacred spaces such as temples, churches, or shrines.

These places can evoke a sense of peace and spiritual connection, allowing you to deepen your spiritual awareness.

How can I explore different spiritual traditions and beliefs?

You can start by attending workshops or lectures on different spiritual practices, or reading books on various traditions.

Keep an open mind and allow yourself to learn from the wisdom of different cultures and belief systems.

How can I find like-minded individuals in spiritual communities to connect with?

You can seek out spiritual communities such as meditation groups, yoga classes, or spiritual retreats where you can connect with others who share similar beliefs and values.

Joining a local meditation group or attending a spiritual retreat can be a great way to meet others on a similar path and form deep, meaningful connections.

What are other practices besides meditation that can deepen my spiritual connection?

Besides meditation, practices such as yoga, mindfulness, journaling, or energy work can also help deepen your spiritual connection.

These practices can help you develop a deeper sense of awareness and mindfulness, which are key to spiritual growth.

Can deepening my spiritual awareness lead to personal growth and transformation?

Yes, deepening your spiritual awareness can lead to personal growth and transformation.

It can help you gain a deeper understanding of yourself, your purpose, and your place in the world, leading to greater compassion, emotional resilience, and a sense of inner peace.

How can I maintain a sense of spiritual connection during challenging or stressful times?

During challenging or stressful times, you can maintain a sense of spiritual connection by continuing to engage in your spiritual practices, seeking support from your spiritual community, and practicing self-compassion and self-care.

What role does gratitude play in deepening my connection to the universe and experiencing higher spiritual awareness?

Practicing gratitude can help deepen your connection to the universe and experience higher spiritual awareness by promoting a sense of appreciation and mindfulness.

Acknowledging the abundance in your life and expressing gratitude can help shift your focus from negativity to positivity.

How can I know if I am making progress in deepening my spiritual connection?

You can know if you are making progress in deepening your spiritual connection by paying attention to your inner experiences, such as increased feelings of peace, clarity, and connection, as well as observing positive changes in your thoughts, emotions, and behaviors toward yourself and others.

As we continue our journey of self-discovery, let's now explore the art of aligning our every move in the next chapter. By finding your true north, you can create a life that is in harmony with your innermost desires and beliefs.

Finding Your True North

THE ART OF ALIGNING YOUR EVERY MOVE

"For we are His workmanship, created in Christ Jesus for good works, which God prepared beforehand that we should walk in them" Ephesians 2:10 NKJV

- Gain clarity on making decisions that resonate with your authentic self.

- Trust your intuition and inner guidance to make aligned decisions.

- Practice self-expression and creativity to honor your authentic self.

- Surround yourself with people who support your journey and encourage you to stay true to your inner purpose.

- Stay true to your values and beliefs to live in alignment with your true North.

Blissful Reflection:

The Secret to Aligning Your Actions with Inner Light

Once upon a time, in a tranquil village nestled beneath the open expanse of the night sky, there lived a wise elder named Samuel.

With kind eyes that shone like glistening stars, Samuel was a beacon of hope and inspiration, his demeanor calm, and his wisdom profound.

Much like the countless stars above, his insights provided guidance to the lost and a sense of wonder to the curious.

His greatest lessons were often shared under the celestial dome, where the infinite seemed graspable, and the heavens whispered secrets to those who dared to listen.

One such lesson began on a clear evening.

Samuel had always found comfort and inspiration in the constellations that adorned the heavens, and, sensing a need for upliftment amongst his people, he gathered the villagers to share their radiant glow.

As they settled onto the soft, grassy earth, Samuel's voice danced on the twilight breeze, sharing the simple, yet profound wisdom of Proverbs 3:5-6 NKJV—

> "Trust in the Lord with all your heart,
> And lean not on your own understanding;
> In all your ways acknowledge Him,
> And He shall direct your paths."

He gently reminded them to place their faith in something greater than themselves, and to let their understanding be not merely of the mind, but of the heart too.

With the night sky as his canvas, Samuel began his tale, relating each star to a dream, a purpose, a silently burning passion within each villager.

Just as stars burn their own paths across the sky, he urged his listeners to pursue their destinies with dedication and grace.

He spoke of the rich diversity of stars, each unique in its radiance, and he likened this symphony of light to the beauty of individual human spirits.

In the various sizes, colors, and luminosities of the stars, Samuel saw a reflection of human diversity—the array of gifts, talents, and strengths that every person brings to the tapestry of life.

Drawing from the essence of Colossians 3:23-24 NKJV— Samuel wove a message of diligence and sincere effort.

> "And whatever you do, do it heartily, as to the Lord and not to
> men, knowing that from the Lord you will receive the reward
> of the inheritance; for you serve the Lord Christ."

His conviction was that in doing so, not only would their tasks become acts of worship, but that they would receive the inheritance of celestial joy.

In urging them to serve with the dedication of servants of Christ, Samuel fostered a profound sense of purpose and fulfillment in labor.

As a gentle breeze stirred through the village, Samuel's voice, filled with affection and empathy, rang true in the hearts of his listeners.

Samuel impressed upon them that within each soul lies a light, unique and strong, waiting to be acknowledged and shown forth.

As he wove personal anecdotes and village lore into his narrative, he illustrated how each person, by staying true to their values and beliefs, has the potential to emit a brilliance found in the authenticity of their inner being.

The villagers, captivated by the sage's words, found themselves reflecting on their contributions to the world.

Each person pondered their potential and recognized the beauty of their light shining as an integral part of creation's grand tapestry.

They realized that by aligning their actions with their inner bliss and tapping into that which made their heart sing, they drew strength from the guiding constellations above.

Embracing their quirks and acknowledging their unique role in the Creator's plan sparked a newfound zest for life within their hearts.

A sense of spiritual oneness washed over the village, as if the Creator's love was a blanket tucking them in for the night. In this unity of purpose, a supportive and cooperative spirit blossomed among them, fostering a bond similar to a family gathered under one roof.

The warmth of this fellowship radiated outward, its glow witnessed in the loving actions and compassionate hearts that marked their daily walk.

With the stars twinkling overhead, Samuel reminded the villagers to give thanks for their existence, their purpose, and the intentional design of the universe.

Each star's distinctiveness was a testament to the Creator's attention to detail and care in crafting the wonders of the cosmos—and the marvel that was each human life.

Gratitude for these divine intricacies fostered a deeper appreciation for life, nurturing joy and purpose in the hearts of all.

As time marched on, the village blossomed like a garden under the stewardship of its inhabitants, each person tending to their patch with love and pride.

In aligning their deeds with their deepest joy, they discovered enrichment, robust relationships, and an unquenchable inner flame.

Their understanding of Samuel's teachings became more profound with each passing season, their lives woven into a tapestry as rich as the night sky itself.

The profound symbolism of the stars remained etched in their collective memory, a constant source of inspiration and hope.

Amidst the vastness of the universe, they reveled in their own light's capacity to shine, embracing Samuel's words.

The principles gleaned from scripture remained their compass, guiding them towards lives filled with true contentment, purposeful actions, and the bliss found within.

Samuel's legacy lived on in the hearts of the villagers, a cherished gift that continued to illuminate their paths.

They reveled in the light of their stars, their individuality a cherished treasure, each one contributing to the cosmic dance overhead.

As each night came, the villagers looked skyward with hope, reminded that their purpose, like the stars, was a guiding light leading them toward a life of authenticity, joy, and eternal inspiration.

When we align our actions with our inner bliss and purpose, we unearth a wellspring of fulfillment and meaning that infuses our very existence.

This alignment is about listening to the soft whispers of our heart, about paying attention to the dreams that light us up from the inside and give color to our days.

Imagine a life where each step you take is a note in a harmonious melody that sings of your passions and desires.

Such a life is lived with intention and authenticity—where authenticity means bravely letting go of the masks and expectations that muddle our true essence.

As we shed the layers that don't belong to us, we discover a sense of flow where our daily actions become an effortless dance, a dynamic expression of who we truly are.

When we live in alignment with our inner bliss, even the simplest activities brim with joy, turning the mundane into the extraordinary.

The journey to aligning with our inner purpose begins by tending to the quiet place within us that knows joy beyond words.

It is about taking the time to pause in the bustle of life, to listen—to truly listen—to the yearnings of our soul.

Whether through deep reflection, expressive journaling, or stillness in meditation, each practice can serve as a lantern, shedding light on the contours of our deepest fulfillment.

As the picture of what makes us come alive becomes clear, it's crucial to boldly set intentions that move us toward those dreams.

This might mean making courageous choices, like pivoting careers that don't align with our joy, nurturing relationships that allow us to soar, or fostering daily habits that nourish our well-being.

All of these are threads in the tapestry of a life woven with purpose.

And remember, this is not a one-time act but a loving commitment to oneself—a commitment to revisit and realign with our authentic path continually.

It's about the gentle vigilance in checking that our external actions reflect the song our heart wants to sing, ensuring that our light shines undimmed by the transient nature of our external circumstances.

It's not always easy, but the rewards of these practical steps in terms of living a more fulfilling and authentic life are truly priceless.

Step 1: Make Decisions that Resonate with Your Authentic Self

When we embark on the journey of aligning our actions with our inner bliss, we are, in essence, courting our true selves to step into the light.

Making decisions that resonate with your authentic self is quite the art—it requires a harmonious blend of introspection, courage, and self-respect.

It invites you to sink into the quietude of your own being, to engage in a dialogue with your inner voice that sees beyond the superficial desires imprinted by external expectations.

The sweet spot of bliss and fulfillment is uncovered not in the unruly clatter of the world but in the gentle whispers of your soul.

By consciously choosing to engage in activities that evoke joy—be it painting with wild abandon, scribing your thoughts into existence, or flowing through the meditative dances of yoga—you carve out a sanctuary for joy within your everyday life.

These activities become an ode to your essence, a loyal testament to the fact that when you honor your most authentic self, you're building a life that's not only lived but cherished in each vibrant moment.

As you navigate the waters of personal connections, it becomes evident that the fabric of your relationships must be woven with the same threads that match the colors of your own values and needs. If honesty and communication shine as cornerstones in the foundation of your authentic

**self, then it is imperative that your relationships mirror
these virtues.**

It is about cultivating spaces where your truth can breathe unencumbered and where your heart can speak its language without fear.

Decisions in relationships then transform into acts of self-love, ensuring that every connection you nurture is a resonant reflection of your authenticity.

Similarly, when you stand at the career crossroads, let the lantern of your passion light your path.

If the pulse of your satisfaction quickens at the thought of serving and uplifting others, heed the call of careers that echo your heart's desires.

Whether you find solace in the healing arts, satisfaction in the edifying realms of social work, or fulfillment in the act of counseling, the compass of your joy guides you toward professional avenues where every task you undertake is filled with purpose and passion.

Remember, when you align your vocational choices with the authenticity of your spirit, the work you do transcends into a labor of love—a true manifestation of your inner self in harmonious action.

Here are some additional steps:

Reflect on your values and beliefs:

Take the time to understand what truly matters to you and what values guide your life.

This will provide a foundation for making decisions that are in alignment with your authentic self.

Listen to your intuition:

Trust your gut feelings and inner instincts when it comes to making decisions.

Your intuition is often a powerful tool in guiding you toward choices that are right for you.

Consider the impact on your well-being:

Before making a decision, consider how it will impact your overall well-being.

Will it bring you joy, peace, and fulfillment, or will it create stress and discomfort?

Tune into your passions and interests:

Consider what truly excites and energizes you.

Making decisions that align with your passions and interests will bring a sense of purpose and fulfillment to your life.

Practice self-awareness:

Tune into your emotions and feelings to understand how different choices make you feel.

This will help you make decisions that are in line with your authentic self.

Consult with your inner circle:

Seek guidance and support from trusted friends and family members who know you well.

Their insights can help you gain clarity on decisions that align with your true self.

Embrace authenticity:

Be true to yourself, and don't be afraid to make decisions that may go against societal norms or expectations.

Embracing your authentic self is empowering and liberating.

Take time for self-reflection:

Before making a decision, take time to reflect on how it aligns with your core values and beliefs.

This will help you make choices that are in harmony with your authentic self.

Trust in your ability to make decisions:

Believe in your own judgment and trust that you have the wisdom and insight to make choices that resonate with your true self.

Embrace the journey:

Making decisions that align with your authentic self is an ongoing process.

Embrace the journey of self-discovery and growth, knowing that each decision you make is an opportunity to live in alignment with your truest self.

Step 2: Trust Your Intuition and Inner Guidance

Trusting your intuition is similar to having an internal compass that points you toward your true north—where your inner purpose lies.

This compass, often whispering beneath the noise of everyday life, is a formidable ally in your journey toward self-fulfillment.

Whether it's the workplace or your private sphere, intuition acts as a personal guide, a lantern in the fog, illuminating the steps on a path paved with authenticity.

When faced with crucial decisions, be they professional advancements or transitions to new endeavors, allow the quiet confidence of your inner voice to lead the way.

This fidelity to your intuitive self ensures that the actions you take resonate with your deepest aspirations, weaving a narrative of your life that is rich with intention and satisfaction.

Remember, to live a life that is most fulfilling, one must not just listen but also have the courage to act upon the wisdom that emanates from within.

Navigating life's inevitable challenges can be like facing a maze with multiple exits, where trusting your intuition becomes an act of empowerment.

It offers a sense of clarity and direction when crossroads appear, and the map seems to have been blown away by the winds of uncertainty.

By channeling this inner guidance, you approach each hurdle with poise and conviction, making choices that echo your authenticity.

Your intuition becomes the steady pulse guiding your decision-making, ensuring that each step brings you closer to a life replete with purpose and meaning.

The road to developing this trust is intimate and sacred, requiring patience, mindfulness, and repeated ventures into the sanctuary of self-reflection.

Methods such as meditation and journaling serve as conduits to this inner sanctuary, helping silence external distractions and amplify the voice of your inner wisdom.

The more you engage with this personal truth, the more your intuition will emerge as a trusted confidant, encouraging you to embrace its insights across the canvas of your life.

Always remember: when your gut speaks with a heartfelt conviction, honor it with the trust it deserves, and let it sculpt the actions that define your existence.

Here are some additional steps:

Reflect on past experiences where your intuition has guided you in the right direction.

Pay attention to physical sensations and emotions that arise when making decisions.

Practice mindfulness and tune into your inner thoughts and feelings.

Set aside time for quiet reflection and meditation to connect with your inner guidance.

Keep a journal to track any intuitive insights or feelings that arise throughout the day.

Seek out support and guidance from trusted friends or mentors who can help validate your intuition.

Start small by trusting your intuition in low-stakes decisions and observing the results.

Let go of fear and doubt, and embrace the confidence that comes with trusting your inner guidance.

Take action based on your intuition and observe how things unfold.

Reflect on the outcomes of trusting your intuition, and use it as a source of growth and learning.

Step 3: Practice Self-Expression and Creativity

Embracing the joy of self-expression and creativity is similar to embarking on a journey of self-discovery that adds a rich, colorful layer to the tapestry of life.

By carving out moments each day for journaling, painting, or dancing, you offer yourself a treasured opportunity—a sanctuary where the soul can speak in the purest forms of expression.

Journaling allows you to traverse the landscapes of your inner world, capturing the essence of your thoughts and emotions onto a canvas of words.

Painting invites you to splash your inner visions across a visual expanse, marrying colors and shapes to depict your inner truth.

Dancing, on the other hand, is a rhythmic exploration of freedom, every movement a stroke of authenticity and raw, powerful storytelling.

This daily ritual becomes a nurturing garden where the seeds of personal growth are planted, watered, and blossomed.

Each creative act, a whisper from your core, forges a deeper connection with the numerous facets that compose your being, granting you a sense of clarity and purpose as you express what cannot be said in mere words alone.

Turning to new hobbies and interests further amplifies this expansive palette of self-expression.

Imagine holding a camera for the first time, its lens the eye through which you capture fleeting moments of beauty, teaching you to see the world through a fresh, invigorated perspective.

With each snapshot, you crystallize memories, feelings, and a distinctive intimacy with your surroundings.

Each new hobby is a key unlocking doors to rooms within yourself yet unexplored, filled with unexpected treasures that, once unveiled, can transform your life with newfound joy and satisfaction.

By embracing the odyssey of continual learning and experience, you stitch together a quilt of diverse skills and passions that not only enhances your life with accomplishment but also inspires a deeper fulfillment.

Surround yourself with a tribe of creatives—people who understand the heartbeat of artistry and whose encouragement acts as the wind beneath your wings.

In such a community, your creative flame is fanned, and camaraderie becomes the chorus that sings you toward boundless expression and infinite possibility.

Here are some additional steps:

Find a quiet, comfortable space where you can freely express yourself without any distractions.

Reflect on the activities or hobbies that bring you joy and allow you to express yourself creatively.

Start engaging in activities such as painting, writing, dancing, singing, or any other form of creative expression that resonates with you.

Allow yourself to make mistakes and embrace imperfection as part of the creative process.

Seek inspiration from other creative individuals or art forms to expand your creative horizons.

Set aside dedicated time each day to practice self-expression and creativity, even if it's just for a few minutes.

Keep a journal or sketchbook to document your thoughts, ideas, and creative endeavors.

Share your creative work with others, whether it's through social media, art galleries, or simply with friends and family.

Embrace the process of self-expression and creativity as a means of self-discovery and personal growth.

Step 4: Surround Yourself with People Who Support Your Journey

Embarking on the voyage toward our dreams, whether it be launching a business venture or chasing creative aspirations, is similar to setting sail on an unpredictable sea.

The ocean of ambition is one where tides of challenge and waves of doubt often buffet us relentlessly.

Yet, in these moments, the presence of supportive companions—friends who double as lighthouses and family that steer us through stormy weather—can be the difference between losing our way and reaching new horizons.

As your ship braves the tempest of entrepreneurship, imagine the chorus of encouragement from loved ones, their constructive critiques refining your strategies, while their unwavering belief armors you against the despair of rough currents.

Celebrations of small victories become shared ports of joy, and the collective strength of your support network can turn the tide, guiding you toward success with unfailing positivity and laser-sharp focus.

Reflecting on personal tales of growth, I recognize the profound influence of my own ensemble of supporters. Venturing into the realm of writing, a path strewn with rejection and the cliffs of creative blocks, I discovered the unparalleled power of encouragement.

The voices of friends who saw the spark of potential in my words and the gentle push from those who challenged me to refine my craft transformed the solitary journey into a shared pilgrimage.

Each word of affirmation, each act of faith during seasons of doubt, became the fuel that propelled me further toward my aspirations of becoming a published author.

Just as a rich soil feeds the roots of a flourishing plant, the nurturing environment crafted by your personal cheerleaders allows you to flourish.

The symphony of support goes beyond self; it creates an echo chamber of positivity where ambitions are nurtured, successes are amplified, and the collective charge towards excellence transforms an individual quest into a collective adventure peppered with joy, tenacity, and camaraderie.

<u>Here are some additional steps:</u>

Identify the individuals in your life who consistently show support and encouragement toward your goals and aspirations.

Communicate with these individuals and express your gratitude for their ongoing support and belief in your journey.

Seek out like-minded individuals who share similar goals and aspirations, and create a supportive network of individuals who understand and empathize with your journey.

Limit interactions with individuals who are unsupportive or negative towards your goals, and instead, prioritize spending time with those who uplift and energize you.

Share your progress and achievements with your support system, and celebrate your successes together.

Seek out mentors and role models who have achieved success on similar paths, and learn from their experiences and advice.

Create a positive and uplifting environment by surrounding yourself with affirmations, vision boards, and other visual reminders of your goals.

Attend workshops, events, and seminars where you can connect with individuals who have similar ambitions and can provide valuable insights and advice.

Be open to feedback and constructive criticism from your support system, as they can help you course-correct and stay aligned with your purpose.

Continuously nurture and invest in your relationships with those who support your journey, and reciprocate by offering your support and encouragement in return.

Step 5: Stay True to Your Values and Beliefs

Living in harmony with your values and beliefs imparts a profound sense of agreement between your inner purpose and your outward actions.

It's similar to possessing a compass that unfailingly points you toward authenticity.

When you steadfastly adhere to these personal tenets, every step you take resonates with the essence of who you truly are.

Consider a scenario where a course of action conflicts with your deeply held convictions.

Such crossroads are invitations to pause and recalibrate, to weigh the superficial allure of convenience against the enduring satisfaction of staying aligned with what you hold dear.

Forging a path that reflects your inner convictions may not always be the easiest route, but it's the one that allows you to look back with pride, knowing you lived a life that was genuine and true to yourself.

In the professional realm, say you're faced with a choice that tests your moral fiber. Upholding your principles might invite criticism or pose risks, but it reinforces the integrity that forms the bedrock of your character.

For instance, by advocating for fairness in the face of injustice, you not only solidify your own standing but may also galvanize others to heed their moral callings.

Within the sphere of personal relationships, consider the dynamic with a friend whose actions negate the uplifting and positive engagements you cherish.

Addressing this misalignment head-on isn't just about establishing boundaries; it fosters an environment conducive to mutual growth and respect, illuminating the strength of character that lies in compassionate truth-telling.

Embarking on the journey of aligning your existence with your inner joy and purpose means not only making choices that resonate with your true self but also cultivating intuition, creative expression, a community of support, and unwavering dedication to your ideals.

This alignment carves out a life complete with fulfillment, intentionality, and an unshakeable bond to your core identity – a narrative authored by none other than you.

Here are some additional steps:

Reflect on your core values and beliefs to identify your true North.

Take time to understand your passions and desires in life.

Define your long-term goals and what success looks like for you.

Evaluate your current actions and decisions to see if they align with your true North.

Identify any areas in your life where you may be straying from your true North.

Create a plan for realigning your actions and decisions with your true North.

Seek out support and guidance from mentors or trusted individuals who can help steer you in the right direction.

Practice mindfulness and self-awareness to stay grounded.

Make adjustments as necessary to keep yourself on track.

Regularly reassess and realign your actions to ensure you are constantly moving toward your true North.

Ways of Alignment:

Self-reflection:

Take time to reflect on your values, beliefs, and goals to gain a clearer understanding of who you are and what is important to you.

Identify your core values:

Determine what principles and values are most important to you and align with your true self.

Set meaningful goals:

Define specific, actionable goals that align with your values and will lead you toward your true North.

Tune into your inner compass:

Pay attention to your instincts and intuition to guide your decisions and actions in alignment with your true North.

Seek clarity:

Engage in practices such as meditation or journaling to gain clarity and insight into your purpose and direction.

Surround yourself with supportive people:

Build a network of people who support and encourage you in your journey to align with your true North.

Practice authenticity:

Strive to be genuine and true to yourself in all aspects of your life, from your relationships to your career choices.

Embrace growth and change:

Be open to evolving and adapting as you continue to align with your true North and pursue your goals.

Take inspired action:

Use your intuition and inner guidance to take steps toward your goals and make decisions that align with your true North.

Reflect and adjust:

Regularly assess your progress and make adjustments as needed to ensure that you are continually aligning with your true North.

Chapter Summary

- Make decisions that resonate with your authentic self

- Trust your intuition and inner guidance

- Practice self-expression and creativity

- Surround yourself with people who support your journey

- Stay true to your values and beliefs

FAQ

How can I make decisions that resonate with my authentic self?

To make decisions that resonate with your authentic self, take the time to listen to your inner voice and pay attention to what truly brings you joy and fulfillment.

Honor the truth of what brings you happiness and make decisions in alignment with it.

Why is trusting your intuition and inner guidance important in aligning your actions with your inner purpose?

Trusting your intuition and inner guidance is important because they can guide you toward choices and actions that will bring you the most fulfillment.

Your intuition is a powerful tool that can help you stay aligned with your inner purpose.

Why is staying true to my values and beliefs essential in aligning my actions with my inner purpose?

Staying true to your values and beliefs is essential because it helps you live in alignment with your true self.

When you honor and uphold your core values and beliefs, you are staying true to your inner purpose.

How can I identify my core values and beliefs?

You can identify your core values and beliefs by reflecting on what truly matters to you in life.

Think about the principles and ideals that are most important to you, and consider how they align with your actions and decisions.

How can I develop and strengthen my intuition to better guide my actions?

To develop and strengthen your intuition, take time for quiet reflection and meditation.

Pay attention to the signals and feelings that arise within you when making decisions, and trust the guidance that comes from within.

What are some practical steps for staying true to my values and beliefs in my daily life?

Some practical steps for staying true to your values and beliefs in your daily life include setting clear boundaries, making decisions that align with your principles, and surrounding yourself with like-minded individuals who support and understand your beliefs.

Now that we've learned the art of aligning our every move, let's shift our focus to embracing setbacks as stepping stones to success in the next chapter. It's time to discover the upside of down and find the inspiration and resilience to overcome obstacles on our journey toward achieving our goals.

The Upside of Down

EMBRACING SETBACKS AS STEPPING STONES TO SUCCESS

"The LORD is my strength and my shield; my heart trusts in Him, and He helps me. My heart leaps for joy, and with my song I praise him."
- Psalm 28:7 NIV

- Approach obstacles with a positive mindset, reframing them as opportunities for growth and learning.

- Learn from setbacks and failures, taking the time to reflect on valuable lessons and what you can do differently in the future.

- Seek support when facing difficulties, whether it's from friends, family, or a support group, to provide the encouragement and guidance needed to navigate through tough times.

- Stay resilient and persevere through adversity by cultivating resilience through practicing self-care, maintaining a positive outlook, and staying focused on your goals.

- Use challenges as a catalyst for personal development, embracing the opportunity for growth and seeing setbacks as a chance to become the best version of yourself.

Blissful Reflection:

The Village Nobleman's Powerful Message Will Change the Way You View Setbacks and Trials Forever

In the quaint village nestled among the rolling hills, there lived a nobleman renowned for his impeccable vision.

With the wisdom of someone who had seen much of the world, he had a certain clarity of thought that cast light onto the simplest of matters, making them seem profound.

One winter's day, as the villagers bustled about their chores, the nobleman called them to gather in the square.

He held up a delicate snowflake, letting the sunlight dance upon its crystalline structure.

The villagers, drawn by curiosity, formed a circle around him. "Behold," he said with a gentle voice, "each one of these snowflakes is a masterpiece, unique and irreplaceable. Just as each snowflake holds its own exquisite design, so too does each one of us."

His words were like a soothing balm, urging each listener to recognize their beauty and worth, a message sent to stir the soul and inspire the heart to embrace its individuality as God's masterpieces.

The nobleman's message resonated deeply within the villagers, stirring their hearts and igniting a sense of wonder within them.

He spoke of the care with which each snowflake was formed, a symbol of God's intricate design in creating every human being with a distinctive purpose.

He related this to the grand tapestry of life, where every thread, every person, is essential to the complete picture.

How vital it was, he emphasized, to embrace the setbacks and trials they faced, acknowledging them not as stumbling blocks but as vital stepping stones.

It was these very challenges, the nobleman professed, that would mold them into the resilient and compassionate individuals God intended them to be—a message that glistened with the promise of growth and the beauty of transformation.

His teachings were not merely his own but echoed the everlasting wisdom of the scriptures, bringing them to life in a way that resonated with every heart in attendance.

He shared tales and Bible verses, and as the nobleman described the strength and perseverance born of adversity, he reminded the villagers of James 1:2-4 NIV—

> "Consider it pure joy, my brothers and sisters, whenever you face trials of many kinds, because you know that the testing of your faith produces perseverance. Let perseverance finish its work so that you may be mature and complete, not lacking anything."

The verse urged them to consider it pure joy when they encountered obstacles, for the testing of their faith through such trials nurtures perseverance.

In this way, he showed them that the hardships they endure have the power to fortify their spirits just as the snowflake endures the storm, becoming only more resplendent in its journey.

He went on to share the scripture from Hebrews 12:11 NIV—

> "No discipline seems pleasant at the time, but painful. Later on, however, it produces a harvest of righteousness and peace for those who have been trained by it."

Instilling in them the understanding that while discipline may seem difficult at the moment, it bears the peaceful fruit of righteousness for those who are trained by it.

This insightful lesson urged the villagers to endure the rigors of life with the knowledge that their toils were not in vain but were instead cultivating a harvest of virtue and tranquility within their souls.

As the sun dipped below the horizon, painting the sky in hues of orange and purple, the villagers left with a new perspective on life's troubles.

Their steps were lighter, their hearts filled with a newfound appreciation for their individual journeys.

They now understand that every moment of difficulty was an opportunity to aspire to greater heights, to strengthen their resolve, and to grow in character and faith.

With gratitude now blooming in their hearts, they embraced their peculiarities and their purpose.

They did this with the joyful acknowledgment that each of them was crafted with God's loving attention to detail, just as the snowflake was made uniquely beautiful in its own right.

The message began to take root, transforming their view of themselves and the world around them.

As night settled upon the village, the nobleman's profound insights blossomed within the hearts of the villagers.

The scripture from Romans 5:3-5 NIV–

> "Not only so, but we also glory in our sufferings, because we know that suffering produces perseverance; perseverance, character; and character, hope. And hope does not put us to shame,

because God's love has been poured out into our hearts through the Holy Spirit, who has been given to us."

This verse became their strength, as they learned to take pride in their sufferings, knowing that such experiences breed perseverance.

Perseverance, in turn, forges character, and from character springs hope—a hope that is never in vain, for it is anchored in the love God has poured into their hearts through the Holy Spirit.

Inspired by the nobleman's teachings, the villagers began to live out each day with a newfound zeal for life.

They celebrated their uniqueness and found solace even amidst trials.

Philippians 4:13 NKJV—

"I can do all things through Christ who strengthens me."

instilled within them the confidence that they could face any challenge through the strength Christ provided,

while 2 Timothy 4:7 NIV—

" I have fought the good fight, I have finished the race, I have kept the faith."

reminded them of the victory found in maintaining faith through life's race.

Theirs was a daily practice of living with purpose, inspired by a divine narrative.

Change rippled through the old village like a fresh breeze, as the once uncertain and weary residents found themselves uplifted, charged with motivation and inspiration.

The nobleman's words had sparked a flame within them that would not be extinguished—a flame of hope and determination.

Adversities did not cease, for such is the way of life, but the villagers met each challenge with a fierce resolve born of their newfound wisdom.

They learned the power of tenacity and the strength found in unity, drawing from the faith that had been nurtured in their collective heart.

They faced their trials head-on, emerging each time with a resilience that surprised even themselves.

And so, as the villagers moved forward through the seasons of life, they did so with a conviction in the power of the human spirit.

They knew that they were *"fearfully and wonderfully made,"* as the Psalmist says, capable of embracing their unique designs with confidence.

In the light of God's love, they flourished, growing not only in stature but in spirit—a testament to the transformative power of recognizing oneself as God's own masterpiece.

Embracing challenges and setbacks as opportunities for growth is similar to stepping into a forge where character is both tested and strengthened.

As heavy as the hammer of adversity may strike, it is through these very blows that our resolve can be shaped into something more durable and exquisite.

Imagine facing obstacles not as impassable mountains but as rugged paths leading to new outlooks of self-discovery and competence.

When we wade into difficulties with a mindset armored in positivity, we build a formidable resilience.

This resilience does more than merely shield us—it propels us forward, transmuting trials into triumphs and breeding determination that becomes unyielding in the face of future strife.

The metamorphosis from enduring to thriving begins with a simple yet profound shift in perception: every challenge is a mentor in disguise, every setback a curriculum for excellence.

Yet even the mightiest of heroes know that wisdom lies in seeking counsel and camaraderie amidst the battle.

Comrades in the form of friends, family, or mentors can be the torchbearers in the tunnels of our tribulations, illuminating hidden pathways and warming the chill of doubt with their supportive glow.

They remind us that the weight of the world need not rest solely upon our own shoulders; a shared burden is lighter to bear.

As we unearth the immense power nestled within our trials, we convert the energy of struggle into stepping stones toward the success that awaits us.

Walking alongside those who can echo our optimism and infuse us with fresh insights will not only bolster our spirits but also guide our steps more surely across the challenging terrains we traverse.

To reframe adversity as a portal to growth is like finding the secret script of life, where every setback is a plot twist elevating the hero's journey.

With these practical steps and the right mindset and support system in place, you can turn setbacks into stepping stones that propel you toward your goals.

Step 1: Approach Obstacles with a Positive Mindset

The secret to transforming setbacks into stepping stones is rooted in embracing a positive mindset.

It is imperative to shift from perceiving challenges as debilitating roadblocks to recognizing them as fertile grounds for learning and growth.

For example, when a work project veers off course, instead of being bogged down by frustration, reframe your perspective and view this as an invaluable chance to acquire new skills or innovate your strategies.

Let the disappointment fuel your curiosity and drive you to explore alternative solutions, paving the way for professional development and enhanced problem-solving capabilities.

Cultivating such a mindset ensures that you not only bounce back from these setbacks but also ascend to higher levels of success and proficiency.

When facing a difficult setback, like the sting of a failed exam or the heartache of rejection, your instinct might be to retreat into hopelessness.

Yet, it is precisely in these trials of disappointment that a positive mindset can be transformative.

Resist the urge to wallow in what went wrong and, instead, channel your energy into harvesting lessons from the experience.

Every failure is ripe with wisdom, every rejection a guidepost redirecting your journey.

By choosing optimism and resilience, you champion a mindset that not only navigates the chaos of the present but also strengthens you for future endeavors.

Embrace each challenge with a resilient spirit, and you'll find that your journey—strewn with setbacks—is, in fact, a medley of growth, strength, and unrelenting determination.

Here are some additional steps:

Recognize the obstacle:

Identify the specific challenge or setback you are facing.

Change your perspective:

Shift your mindset from seeing the obstacle as a barrier to seeing it as a chance for personal and professional development.

Practice gratitude:

Focus on the things that are going well in your life and be thankful for them, which can help build a positive mindset.

Reframe your thoughts:

Replace negative thoughts with positive affirmations, such as "I am capable of overcoming this obstacle" or "I will learn and grow from this experience."

Seek support:

Surround yourself with positive and encouraging people who can help you stay optimistic and motivated.

Take small steps:

Break the obstacle down into manageable tasks and focus on making progress one step at a time.

Accept mistakes:

Understand that setbacks are a natural part of the learning process and use them as opportunities to improve.

Visualize success:

Imagine yourself overcoming the obstacle and achieving your goals, which can help maintain a positive mindset.

Stay resilient:

Keep pushing forward and remain resilient in the face of challenges, knowing that setbacks are temporary and can be overcome.

Celebrate progress:

Acknowledge and celebrate the small victories along the way, which can help reinforce a positive mindset and keep you motivated.

Step 2: Learn from Setbacks and Failures

Setbacks and failures are not the end of the road; they are part of the journey that molds us into wiser and more resilient individuals.

Whenever we falter, it's essential to take a step back and analyze the situation.

Reflecting on a personal disappointment, such as a failed relationship, means digging deep into what has transpired to gather insights into ourselves.

What aspects of the relationship could have been better? What have you discovered about your needs and boundaries?

Learning from these experiences provides a foundation for future relationships, guiding us on how to build them on stronger, more understanding grounds.

Take, for instance, when I underperformed in a critical case study presentation.

Initially engulfed by frustration, I took a moment to introspect and recognized my shortcomings – inadequate preparation and the dismissal of valuable insights from peers.

This epiphany reinforced the significance of diligence and embracing constructive feedback – two pivotal pillars I now uphold in all my undertakings.

Engaging in such reflective exercises turns apparent failures into lessons that fuel personal growth and success.

Life's hurdles are inevitable; it is how we respond to them that truly defines our character.

I recall traversing through a turbulent phase in my personal life where all seemed lost, and defeat felt certain.

But amidst the chaos, I chose to seek the silver lining.

This period of tribulation became a transformative experience, instilling in me the virtues of resilience and patience.

It highlighted the importance of community and the strength drawn from reaching out for support in despairing times.

The ordeal didn't just toughen my spirit; it expanded my capacity for empathy, enabling me to connect with and support others in their moments of distress.

Equipped with these insights, the conviction to persist in the darkest of times solidified within me.

As I navigated through subsequent challenges, I turned to see not roadblocks, but stepping stones leading toward greater victories.

Each stumble and fall has been a lesson in perseverance, adaptability, and maintaining a positive outlook.

These setbacks have been invaluable in sculpting a more tenacious, resourceful, and optimistic person who stands before life's adversities, ready to rise and push forward.

Embrace your setbacks and wear them as badges of honor, as they are fertile ground for cultivating your best self.

Here are some additional steps:

Acknowledge the setback or failure and allow yourself to feel any emotions that come with it.

Take a step back and analyze the situation objectively to understand what exactly went wrong.

Identify the specific factors that contributed to the setback or failure.

Take responsibility for your own role in the situation and avoid placing blame on others.

Consider alternative approaches or strategies that could have led to a different outcome.

Seek feedback from trusted sources to gain different perspectives on the situation.

Use the experience as an opportunity for growth and personal development.

Develop a plan for how you can apply the lessons learned to future situations.

Stay resilient and maintain a positive mindset as you move forward from the setback or failure.

Keep an open mind and be willing to try new approaches in the future based on the lessons learned.

Step 3: Seek Support when Facing Difficulties

In times of adversity, asking for support is not just important—it is a testament to your resilience.

The act of reaching out connects your journey to others, turning solitary struggles into shared experiences.

Friends and family become beacons of hope, affirming that you don't have to face challenges alone.

Within their words of encouragement lies a power that can transform your outlook, making obstacles seem more doable.

Similarly, turning to people who have weathered similar storms, like mentors or career coaches, can illuminate the path forward, offering tailored advice born from lived experience.

These guides offer more than wisdom—they serve as living proof that overcoming hardships is possible.

Your support system is a reflection of the positive forces in your life, and embracing it reveals your commitment to personal growth.

Tapping into this network is a brave step that underscores your determination to improve your circumstances.

Sharing your story with others who empathize can be incredibly therapeutic, fortifying your resolve to press on.

Support groups, whether woven into the fabric of your local community or found in the digital realm, are reservoirs of collective strength.

These are spaces where triumph and trouble intermingle, creating a mosaic of human experience that reminds us of our shared humanity.

By inviting assistance and being surrounded by those who champion your success, you enable hope to thrive amidst hardship.

Remember, seeking help is a courageous endeavor, a clear sign of your unwavering spirit, not a surrender to weakness.

Embrace the help offered by those who care, and step forward with confidence, knowing you are never truly alone in your journey.

Here are some additional steps:

Recognize and acknowledge that you are facing difficulties and that it's okay to ask for help.

Identify who in your support network you can reach out to for assistance.

Schedule a time to talk with the person or group you've chosen to seek support from.

Be honest and open about the challenges you are facing and your feelings about them.

Listen to the advice and guidance offered by your support network and consider how it can be applied to your situation.

Keep an open mind and be willing to try new approaches or perspectives on your difficulties.

Take the time to process and reflect on the support and advice you've received.

Check-in regularly with your support network to provide updates and seek additional assistance as needed.

Express gratitude to those who have offered their support and guidance.

Be open to offering support to others in return, creating a reciprocal and supportive environment within your network.

Step 4: Stay Resilient and Persevere Through Adversity

Resilience is not just a trait but a transcendent force that enables us to overcome the inevitable trials and tribulations of life.

It is the innate capacity to rebound from adversity, to adapt, and to keep pressing onward toward our dreams, even when the terrain of existence turns difficult.

To harness this unconquerable spirit, it's paramount to engage in self-care rituals that nourish both body and soul, fostering a sanctuary of positivity from which to draw strength.

Like a sapling that bends in the storm but does not break, we too, must maintain a positive outlook; it is the sunlight that nourishes our growth, even amidst the shadows.

Goals, our north stars, guide us through the fog of uncertainty, providing direction when the path becomes unclear.

By reminding ourselves of past triumphs and our unique reservoir of talents, we can shed the weight of doubt and rekindle the inner flame that whispers, "Keep moving forward."

When life throws unpleasant experiences, it can be all too tempting to gaze into the abyss of discouragement.

Yet, it is in these very moments that the essence of resilience becomes most apparent.

See each challenge as a teacher, each obstacle a stepping stone on the pathway to wisdom.

By keeping the fires of a positive outlook well-tended, we illuminate the road ahead, turning what may seem like impassable hurdles into challenges within our power to conquer.

Possessing the knowledge that our capabilities are as vast as the ocean – deep and swarming with untapped potential – we can sail bravely into the storm.

Staying grounded in consistent personal rituals such as mindfulness meditation or engaging in regular physical activity can be our anchor, stabilizing us in turbulent seas.

Let us not forget the shared human journey either - spending time with loved ones, sharing battles, and celebrating victories enhances our resilience.

Every goal attained is a testament to perseverance, reinforcing our ability to reach further and dream bigger.

Thus, in cultivating a mindset steeped in optimism, self-care, and unwavering focus on our goals, we ready ourselves to face any challenge that dares to impede our voyage.

Resilience is a gift—a sacred key we all hold, capable of unlocking doors to unimagined possibilities and heightened strength with every rebound.

Here are some additional steps:

Recognize setbacks as part of the natural journey toward success.

Embrace the learning opportunities that come with setbacks.

Reflect on the lessons and insights gained from setbacks.

Set new goals and create a plan for moving forward.

Use setbacks as motivation to push harder and work smarter.

Seek support and guidance from mentors or trusted individuals.

Cultivate resilience and a positive mindset to overcome setbacks.

Take calculated risks and embrace the unknown.

Celebrate small victories and progress made along the way.

Use setbacks as stepping stones to ultimately achieve success.

Step 5: Use Challenges as a Catalyst for Personal Development

Challenges are the unseen hands that sculpt our character, forging resilience out of the fires of adversity.

Embarking on the journey of life, it's crucial to remember that hurdles are not meant to stop us in our tracks, but rather to be the whetstone that sharpens our will.

Perceiving each difficulty as a lesson awaiting to be unlocked transforms what could be a stagnant barrier into a motivator, prompting us to expand our horizons and explore the strength within.

It is through the relentless act of pushing past what we once deemed impossible that we encounter the essence of growth, channeling our potential into becoming more formidable individuals.

The art of flourishing during adversity is not just about survival; it's an invitation to step into a realm of self-discovery, to find pride in our ability to persevere, and to acknowledge that within every challenge lies the seed of our future greatness.

Approaching life's detours with an optimistic spirit is similar to navigating a maze with the assurance of hidden treasures along the way.

Each bump in the road is a unique narrative of triumph waiting to be written, enticing us to rise above our limitations and author a tale of personal victory.

By taking setbacks as time for reflection, we uncover insights that show us how to dance in the rain instead of just sitting around waiting for the storm to pass.

This proactive stance not only diminishes the shadows cast by tribulations but also illuminates the path forward, guiding us toward a resilience that is as unyielding as it is graceful.

So let us wear our scars as badges of honor, as celebratory marks of the distinct journey each of us undertakes.

May we transform adversity into a launchpad, propelling us not just toward success but toward a more profound, invincible version of ourselves that can only emerge through the trials of life's challenges.

Here are some additional steps:

Acknowledge the adversity:

Recognize and acknowledge the challenge or setback you are facing, and accept that it may be difficult to overcome.

Practice self-care:

Take care of your physical, emotional, and mental health by getting enough rest, eating well, and seeking support from friends and loved ones.

Maintain a positive mindset:

Focus on the things that are within your control and try to find the silver lining in difficult situations.

Set realistic goals:

Break down your larger goals into smaller, achievable steps, and celebrate each small victory along the way.

Stay flexible:

Be open to adapting your plans and strategies as needed in response to changing circumstances.

Seek support:

Don't be afraid to ask for help from others, whether it's for advice, encouragement, or practical assistance.

Keep a routine:

Establishing a regular routine can provide a sense of stability and predictability during challenging times.

Learn from setbacks:

Instead of dwelling on failures, use them as opportunities to learn and grow.

Stay connected:

Maintain connections with friends, family, and other support systems to combat feelings of isolation and loneliness.

Never give up:

Keep moving forward and remind yourself that resilience is a skill that can be cultivated and strengthened over time.

Remember, setbacks and challenges are a natural part of life, but by approaching them with a positive mindset, seeking support, and staying resilient, you can turn them into stepping stones to success.

<u>Ways to Finding Success Through Setbacks:</u>

Acknowledge setbacks as part of the journey toward success.

Reflect on the lessons and insights gained from each setback.

Use setbacks as motivation to push through and overcome obstacles.

Seek support from mentors, peers, and resources to help navigate setbacks.

Take time to reassess goals and strategies in response to setbacks.

Embrace resilience and perseverance in the face of setbacks.

Learn to adapt and pivot in response to unexpected challenges.

Cultivate a positive mindset and focus on the opportunities within setbacks.

Celebrate the small victories and progress made despite setbacks.

Share your experiences and lessons learned with others to inspire and encourage their own journeys toward success.

Chapter Summary

- Approach obstacles with a positive mindset.

- Learn from setbacks and failures.

- Seek support when facing difficulties.

- Stay resilient and persevere through adversity.

- Use challenges as a catalyst for personal development.

FAQ

How can I approach obstacles with a positive mindset?

You can approach obstacles with a positive mindset by reframing them as opportunities for growth and learning.

Instead of seeing challenges as insurmountable roadblocks, try to view them as chances to develop new skills or approaches.

For example, if you encounter a setback at work, such as a project not going as planned, try to see it as an opportunity to learn new skills or a different approach to the project.

How can I learn from setbacks and failures?

You can learn from setbacks and failures by taking the time to reflect on what went wrong and what you can learn from the experience.

For instance, if you face a personal setback, such as a failed relationship, take the opportunity to reflect on what you have learned about yourself and what you can do differently in future relationships.

Where can I seek support when facing difficulties?

You can seek support when facing difficulties from friends, family, or a support group. It's important to reach out for help to receive the encouragement and guidance needed to navigate through tough times.

For example, if you're going through a challenging time in your career, consider seeking guidance from a mentor or career coach to help you find a way forward.

How can I stay resilient and persevere through adversity?

You can stay resilient and persevere through adversity by practicing self-care, maintaining a positive outlook, and staying focused on your goals.

When faced with adversity, remind yourself of your strengths and keep pushing forward, no matter how tough the road may seem.

How can I use challenges as a catalyst for personal development?

You can use challenges as a catalyst for personal development by embracing the opportunity for personal growth and seeing setbacks as a chance to become the best version of yourself.

Each obstacle you overcome can make you stronger, more adaptable, and more resilient.

What are some examples of setbacks as stepping stones to success?

Some examples of setbacks as stepping stones to success could be a failed business venture that teaches valuable lessons for the next venture, a personal failure that leads to self-discovery and personal growth, or a career setback that inspires a new direction in one's professional life.

How can I start reframing setbacks as opportunities for growth?

You can start reframing setbacks as opportunities for growth by consciously changing your mindset and viewing challenges as chances to develop new skills, gain new experiences, and learn from the situation.

How can setbacks be turned into stepping stones to success?

Setbacks can be turned into stepping stones to success by approaching them with a positive mindset, seeking support, learning from the experience, staying resilient, and using challenges as a catalyst for personal development.

These actions can help you grow and ultimately lead to success.

Now that we've learned to embrace setbacks, let's shift our focus to empowerment through authenticity in the next chapter. It's time to celebrate our uniqueness and unleash the unstoppable potential within ourselves.

Unique and Unstoppable

Empowerment Through Authenticity

G od has given each of us a unique design and purpose. Let your light shine, and share your inner bliss with the world. Just as animals exhibit distinctive patterns, embrace your individuality and make a positive impact.

- Inspire and uplift others through your story, connecting with them on a deep, emotional level.

- Create a supportive and inclusive community for like-minded individuals to express themselves authentically.

- Advocate for authenticity and self-expression, speaking out against societal pressures that stifle individuality.

- Be a beacon of positivity and hope for others, influencing them to adopt a more optimistic outlook.

- Encourage individuality and self-discovery in others, helping them unlock their potential and live more fulfilling lives.

Blissful Reflection:

The Garden of Individuality: How Embracing Quirks Can Transform the World

In a tranquil village cradled by green hills, there was a resplendent garden that was a feast for the senses.

The garden boasted a dizzying array of lush flowers, plant life, and lively animals, each contributing its own harmony to the chorus of nature.

It captured the imagination of the villagers, who often paused to admire the multitude of life forms thriving together.

It was within this serene area that the garden's caretaker, a woman graced with kindness and wisdom, offered an invitation to the villagers to join her in the heart of this earthly paradise for the sharing of a heartfelt story.

As the gathering commenced, the caretaker led the villagers through the garden's many paths.

"Behold," she spoke with a gentle voice, guiding them to witness the subtle beauty concealed within each leaf's vein, the riot of color unfolding in the petals of flowers, and the rich tapestry woven by the garden's wildlife.

"Do you see how every pattern, every hue, every creature is distinct and yet belongs here?" she asked.

Her question hung in the air, reflecting the unity among diversity and hinting at a deeper knowledge.

The caretaker wished to illustrate a profound truth: that each of us is a unique masterpiece in life's great canvas, adored by the Creator for our remarkable differences.

Our eyes, mirrors to the soul, hold the complexity and splendor of being wonderfully made.

Drawing from the wellspring of wisdom found in the scriptures, the caretaker recounted the words of Psalm 139:14 NIV—

"I praise you because I am fearfully and wonderfully made; your works are wonderful, I know that full well."

She wove this message with Matthew 5:14 NIV—

"You are the light of the world. A town built on a hill cannot be hidden,"

And 1 Corinthians 12:4-6 NKJV—

"There are diversities of gifts, but the same Spirit. There are differences of ministries, but the same Lord. And there are diversities of activities, but it is the same God who works all in all."

celebrating the varied gifts bestowed by a singular Spirit.

The assembled villagers listened, enveloped in a sense of awe, as these words painted a vision of individual significance and divine craftsmanship.

With the scripture fresh in their minds, she shared a deeply personal tale.

Her journey of self-discovery had been an embrace of her intrinsic individuality and the acknowledgment of her unique role within God's grand scheme.

In doing so, she had found her calling: to be a torchbearer of authenticity, guiding others in the village toward the unfiltered expression of their inner selves.

It was a narrative of transformation that humbly inspired, teaching the value of our personal stories in the medley of life.

The caretaker conveyed her message with a compassion that warmed the hearts of her listeners.

She urged them to see the extraordinary within themselves, reminding them that, much like the garden necessitates diverse participants to flourish, their own distinctive qualities were indispensable to the fabric of their community.

In their idiosyncrasies lay potential for greatness, and it was time to honor that truth.

Her words painted a vivid analogy of life's tapestry. Where the garden showcased a multitude of patterns, each villager held a singular purpose, interwoven in a collective destiny.

With this understanding, their combined light could yield a society founded on acceptance and mutual support.

It was in this shared illumination, this collective glow of individual purpose, that the foundation of a nurturing and harmonious community was laid.

Departing the garden, each villager carried with them a seed of enlightenment.

They had discovered a profound connection between the garden's intermixture and their own.

They realized, as they admired the garden's natural tapestry, that their perceived imperfections were, in fact, the roots of their strength.

In celebrating the very things that made them unique, they could spread inspiration and elevate their fellows, much like the assorted beauty of the garden elevated their spirits.

Their experience within the garden had sparked a commitment to serve as beacons of light and hope within their village.

They vowed, with earnest hearts, to honor their unparalleled designs, characterizing them as expressions of an omnipotent love and ingenious creativity.

This acknowledgment fortified their resolve to face the world with renewed positivity.

The verses the caretaker shared offered not only comfort but guidance.

They inspired the villagers to apply their singular talents in uplifting those around them.

They taught that by radiating their inner light and joy, they could contribute to a world filled with kindness and purpose.

It was an invitation to be vessels of compassion, generosity, and goodwill; to share unbound happiness, and to illuminate the world in ways only they could.

Rejuvenated by the caretaker's story, the villagers emerged from the garden with a newfound zest for life.

They vowed to embrace the distinction that marked their existence, committing to lives rich in joy and purpose.

This pledge bound them with an imperishable bond to the universe and kindled a heightened spiritual consciousness.

Thus, the villagers left the garden transformed, bearing the inspired message of the caretaker's teachings within them.

She had reminded them that in the intricate design of the universe, every individual, with their quirks and features, was integral.

They walked away under the banner of this powerful creed, prepared to live authentically, to love wholly, and to spread the light of their unique essence to the far corners of the world.

In a world that often prizes conformity, honoring your unique self is a quiet yet powerful rebellion.

Each of us carries a mixture of life experiences and dreams that, when genuinely expressed, contribute to the rich tapestry of human diversity.

There's an undeniable strength in authenticity—it's like a beacon that not only lights your own path but also guides others in finding their way.

Consider your individuality as both a gift and a mission.

This mission involves stepping into the light, showing your true colors, and in doing so, you offer permission for others to do the same.

By rejecting the confines of 'fitting in,' you carve out spaces for innovation, creativity, and progress.

Remember, your authenticity isn't just about you; it carries the potential to liberate and inspire those around you.

It encourages a world less concerned with masks and more welcoming of the wonderful quirks and intricacies that make us who we are.

Yet, understanding and embracing our authenticity is just the starting point—nurturing it into full bloom is another journey altogether.

To cultivate unwavering self-confidence, start by recognizing and celebrating your small victories.

When self-doubt creeps in, remind yourself of the times you've overcome challenges by relying on your unique abilities.

Setting clear boundaries is another cornerstone in honoring your personal identity.

It means learning to say 'no' to situations that drain your spirit and 'yes' to those that resonate with your core.

Regular self-care rituals are transformative; they allow you to ground yourself and reconnect to your values within everyday noise.

Share your journey with others—not as an act of self-indulgence—but as a beacon for those still navigating their own self-acceptance journey.

By courageously lifting the veil on your struggles and triumphs, you light up a pathway for collective empowerment and a brighter, more authentic society.

By taking these steps and offering actionable advice, we can empower individuals to take positive steps toward being authentic and unstoppable in a world that often pressures them to conform.

Step 1: Inspire and Uplift Others Through Your Story

At the heart of personal growth and self-acceptance lies a seemingly daunting challenge: the fear of being oneself in a world that relentlessly pushes for conformity.

But there is a beacon of hope in this journey, a simple yet profound method to pave the way to genuine self-expression—sharing our personal stories and examples.

Each narrative we offer becomes a thread in a tapestry of human experience, revealing patterns of pain, triumph, and, most importantly, relatable truth.

When we open up and recount our own battles with apprehension, something magical happens. We forge connections, not just with others, but with the hidden aspects of our inner selves.

Our stories, loaded with our unique struggles and victories, serve as a source of solace and camaraderie for those who listen.

Picture someone who is struggling with their identity, tight in the grip of loneliness, now suddenly feeling a warm embrace from a community of voices saying, "I've been there; you are not alone."

This solidarity is a powerful catalyst for change.

By relinquishing our masks and sharing our authentic selves, we grant permission to others to explore their true nature.

It is a gentle nudge, an encouragement that they, too, can walk a path that celebrates who they genuinely are.

Witnessing a person free from the shackles of fear, fully embracing who they are, acts as a beacon that guides others through their storms of self-doubt.

It's an unspoken invitation that whispers in the winds of change, telling tales of liberation and self-discovery.

People are naturally drawn to stories of transformation, and, through these narratives, they elicit the courage needed to face their own fears.

It's as if each story whispers to their soul, urging them to break free from their self-imposed restraints and fully embrace the beautiful complexity of their being.

It's not just about telling our stories; it's about how we tell them.

An approachable, sincere manner invites others to lower their guard, and fosters trust and openness.

When we convey our experiences with warmth and approachability, we create an environment ripe for connection and empathy.

We become living proof that vulnerability is not a weakness but a strength, and that in the tender soil of honesty, the seeds of self-acceptance can flourish.

By sharing ourselves with humility and a dash of vulnerability, we enlighten paths once dim.

We become lighthouses for those navigating the rugged coastline of identity—a friendly beacon reassuring travelers that safe shores are within reach.

Our stories become both a map and a compass, highlighting the rocky terrains we've traversed and pointing towards the horizon of possibilities that lie ahead.

In doing so, we demonstrate that the journey to ourselves doesn't have to be in solitude, but rather a shared expedition enriched by the wisdom and camaraderie of fellow sojourners.

The beauty of personal storytelling is its inherent capacity to create a mosaic of human experience—one that is colorful, diverse, and resonant with the echoes of shared humanity.

Our stories hold a mirror up to the world, reflecting the diversity of life and offering a multitude of perspectives.

They carry the inspirational message that while our stories are uniquely our own, the themes of courage, hope, and self-discovery bind us together.

They illuminate the common ground we share and remind us that our individuality is not a barrier, but a bridge to a more connected and compassionate world.

In essence, the act of sharing our personal stories and examples is both instructional and transformative.

It directs us towards the liberation of self, teaching us by example that we, too, can step into the light of authenticity.

As we listen to and recount tales of bravery and self-love, we are engaged in a dance of mutual upliftment—each step forward, a stride toward a more open-hearted existence.

So let us continue to share, continue to inspire, and continue to guide one another with stories that affirm: being unapologetically yourself is not only possible, but a profound journey worthy of embracing.

<u>Here are some additional steps:</u>

Reflect on your own journey and identify the key moments and experiences that have shaped who you are today.

Consider the impact of your story and how it can resonate with others who may be facing similar challenges or seeking inspiration.

Find a medium through which you can share your story, whether it's through writing, public speaking, or creating visual content.

Craft your narrative in a way that is authentic and relatable, highlighting both the struggles and triumphs that have defined your journey.

Share specific lessons and insights that you have gained from your experiences, offering practical advice and guidance to those who may be in need of support.

Be vulnerable and open about your own vulnerabilities and setbacks, showing that resilience and growth are possible for anyone.

Engage with your audience and create opportunities for dialogue and connection, allowing others to share their own stories and find solidarity in their experiences.

Offer encouragement and hope to those who may be feeling discouraged or disheartened, reminding them that they are not alone in their struggles.

Amplify the voices of others who have also overcome adversity and found purpose and fulfillment in their lives, showcasing a diverse range of inspiring stories.

Continuously seek ways to uplift and empower others through your storytelling, recognizing the positive impact that sharing your journey can have on the world.

Step 2: Create a Supportive and Inclusive Community

Building a community of like-minded individuals is similar to fashioning a rich array of unique threads, each contributing to the overall beauty of the piece.

This environment becomes a treasure trove, where your uniqueness isn't merely appreciated—it's celebrated.

Imagine a space where you can peel away the layers of facade enforced by the broader society and reveal the core of your true self, unfiltered and radiant.

In this community, you find not just acceptance, but a profound understanding that resonates with the very essence of your being.

Here, your personal values aren't up for debate but are the common language spoken by all.

With collective hearts and minds, this group becomes a powerful incubator for personal growth, offering support that is both nourishing and genuine, and encouragement that inspires you to flourish in ways you never thought possible.

To bolster this sense of unity and belonging, consider the power of bringing everyone together through thoughtfully curated events and workshops, or even through vibrant online platforms in this digital age.

These gatherings are more than mere interactions; they're celebrations of individual pathways and shared journeys.

Whether it's an intimate local meetup, an expansive virtual webinar, or a collaborative project, these interactions are opportunities to weave individual strands into a supportive network.

Your objective in creating these spaces is not just to find common ground, but to elevate each unique design, a reminder that the mixture of our collective experiences is made all the more enchanting through diversity.

Engage this community with activities that inspire creativity, spark meaningful conversations, and forge lasting connections.

It's in these shared experiences that the true magic of community is found, and as a leader, your role is to nurture this garden of individuality, encouraging every flower to bloom in its own spectacular way.

Here are some additional steps:

Define the vision and values of the community:

Clearly outline the purpose and core values of the community to ensure alignment among members.

Establish clear communication channels:

Create a platform for open and respectful communication, whether it's through in-person meetings, social media groups, or other channels.

Foster a sense of belonging:

Encourage active participation and create opportunities for members to connect with one another.

Provide resources and support:

Offer resources, guidance, and support for individuals to thrive and contribute to the community.

Educate and raise awareness:

Offer workshops, seminars, or discussions to promote understanding and acceptance of diversity and inclusion within the community.

Embrace diversity:

Encourage the participation of individuals from different backgrounds and perspectives to enrich the community's collective knowledge and experience.

Encourage empathy and respect:

Promote a culture of empathy, understanding, and mutual respect among members.

Address conflicts openly and constructively:

Establish a process for addressing conflicts and differences in a respectful and positive manner to maintain a healthy and supportive community.

Celebrate achievements and milestones:

Recognize and celebrate the accomplishments and milestones of individuals within the community to foster a sense of pride and belonging.

Continuously assess and adapt:

Regularly review the community's progress, gather feedback, and make necessary adjustments to ensure an inclusive and supportive environment for all members.

Step 3: Advocate for Authenticity and Self-Expression

Embarking on the voyage of recognizing and cherishing one's own uniqueness is indeed a remarkable venture into the depths of self-discovery and self-acceptance.

It's about digging deep to uncover the treasure trove of attributes and passions that set you apart from the masses.

Each person is a mosaic of experiences, dreams, and innate talents, and it's the distinct pattern of these pieces that make an individual extraordinary.

Acknowledging this fact is similar to shining a light on your innermost self, creating a luminous pathway for others to follow.

As you journey along this path, remember that the quirks and peculiarities you possess are not just nuances; they are the brushstrokes in the masterpiece that is your life.

Resolve to not only embrace but also celebrate your individuality; understand that you are a garden in bloom, flourishing in a spectrum of colors that contribute to the beauty of diversity in this world.

Yet, this journey is not one to be walked in solitude—it calls for solidarity, for raising our voices in unison for those who are yet to find the strength to stand tall in their own essence.

Life can often feel like a continuous battle against the constricting chains of societal expectations, a world where narrow definitions of beauty and success try to cast unique spirits into a mold that fits all.

Challenge those constraints!

Speak out with kindness and courage, empowering others to join in this tapestry of individuality, demonstrating that success is truly measured by the courage to remain authentic in a world that often rewards conformity.

Mirror the change you wish to see, proving it's not just acceptable, but glorious to be a beacon of originality.

Embrace your own oddities and encourage others to unfold their colors with the same passion.

Create circles of love and acceptance wherever you tread, for it is in these sanctuaries that souls are freed to express their true selves, freed by the shackles of judgment.

Remember, your actions and words have the power to ignite a revolution; a revolution of self-expression, where each person's journey of embracing their uniqueness becomes a collective march toward a world rich in variety and vibrant with the hues of humanity's countless narratives.

<u>**Here are some additional steps:**</u>

Acknowledge the importance of authenticity and self-expression in promoting individuality and diversity.

Educate yourself on the different ways people express themselves, whether through appearance, speech, or actions.

Recognize and challenge any prejudices or stereotypes that might hinder someone's authentic self-expression.

Engage in open and honest conversations with others about the importance of being true to oneself.

Actively listen to others' experiences and struggles with self-expression, and offer support and encouragement.

Speak out against any form of discrimination or judgment that may be directed toward individuals expressing themselves authentically.

Share your own unique experiences and challenges in self-expression to help others feel understood and validated.

Create a safe and inclusive environment where all individuals feel comfortable expressing themselves without fear of judgment or rejection.

Advocate for policies and practices in your community or workplace that promote diversity and inclusivity in self-expression.

Continuously strive to be a positive role model for self-acceptance and authenticity, and encourage others to do the same.

Step 4: Be a Beacon of Positivity and Hope for Others

In times of uncertainty and difficulty, holding the torch of positivity is not just about personal resilience; it's about embodying the hope that fellow travelers along life's winding roads desperately seek.

A genuine smile, an uplifting word, or a steady, confident demeanor can act like a lighthouse guiding ships through a turbulent sea.

Imagine being that steadfast beacon for someone who is buffeted by the gales of doubt or the waves of despair.

Your unwavering optimism is not a naive denial of reality, but rather a powerful testament to the human spirit's capacity to seek out light in the darkest of circumstances.

When you radiate hope, you offer an invisible, yet palpable, lifeline to those who might be on the brink of giving up.

As you traverse your own challenges, remember that your bright outlook on life could be the very thing that helps someone else envision a path forward.

Reflect for a moment on the beauty and transformative power of a kindled spark of positivity.

It begins with a simple gesture or a kind word, but as it spreads from person to person, it grows into a heartwarming blaze that warms the spirits of all it touches.

You, with your repository of uplifting thoughts and your readiness to express them, are more influential than you may realize.

By being the person who cheers on, who validates struggles, and who champions the perseverance of others, you set a magnificent example.

Every act of encouragement fans the flames of courage in someone else.

So go ahead, spread your inspirational energy far and wide. Nourish the roots of optimism in your community.

Let your actions be the ink, writing stories of empowerment and hope.

Never forget: each small act of positivity you radiate is a brushstroke on the canvas of humanity's collective soul, enhancing the picture of our shared existence with the vivid colors of hope and positivity.

<u>Here are some additional steps:</u>

Start each day with a positive mindset, reminding yourself of the blessings and opportunities around you.

Practice gratitude daily, acknowledging the good in your life and expressing appreciation for it.

Be mindful of your words and actions, striving to spread kindness and encouragement wherever you go.

Share your own personal stories of triumph and perseverance to inspire others facing similar challenges.

Offer support and a listening ear to those in need, demonstrating empathy and understanding.

Seek out opportunities to volunteer or contribute to causes that promote hope and positivity in your community.

Surround yourself with uplifting individuals who share your commitment to fostering hope and joy in the world.

Embrace challenges as opportunities for growth, and openly share your experiences and lessons learned with others.

Stay informed about current events and global issues, and look for ways to contribute to solutions that promote positivity and hope.

Reflect on the impact you are making in the lives of others, and continue to strive to be a beacon of positivity and hope in all that you do.

Step 5: Encourage Individuality and Self-Discovery in Others

Embracing and championing the individuality of those around us can ignite a spark of self-discovery that burns brightly within.

When we engage in the powerful act of active listening—to hear the spoken dreams and unvoiced ideas of others—we lay down the bricks of trust and acceptance that pave the road to self-exploration.

Imagine a friend unveiling a newfound interest in art; rather than casting it aside, become the wind beneath their wings.

Ask probing questions that open floodgates of thought: "What moved you towards painting?" "How does it make you feel?"

In doing so, you provide not just an ear, but a mirror for them to see the contours of their unique passions reflected back.

Such validation is potent; it reassures them that their path, though untrodden and distinct, is worth journeying.

Similarly, unveiling the tapestry of our personal journey can stir the souls of others, drawing them magnetically toward their own voyage of self-discovery.

The twists and turns of your narrative may shimmer with lessons and insights that light the way for someone tentatively stepping into their truth.

Say, for instance, your road to self-acceptance was filled with obstacles; sharing this candidly might just be the beacon for someone wrestling with their sense of self.

Your stories can embolden them, invigorating their resolve to assert their individuality in a world that too often champions conformity.

Beyond words, you can become a curator of inspiration, pointing them to books that challenged your perspective, hobbies that unearthed hidden talents, or communities that embraced you, scars and all.

Consider a colleague with a passion for environmental science; you might suggest documentaries on climate change or a collaborative green initiative at work.

This isn't mere assistance; it's an act of empowerment.

Each nudge you provide could be the catalyst transforming a silent wish into a soul-stirring pursuit, enabling them to unravel the rich and complex layers of their existence.

Here are some additional steps:

Listen actively:

Take the time to listen to others without judgment and show genuine interest in their thoughts and feelings.

Acknowledge uniqueness:

Recognize and appreciate the unique qualities and talents of each individual, and let them know that their individuality is valued and respected.

Provide support:

Offer encouragement, guidance, and a safe space for others to explore their true selves and discover their passions.

Offer opportunities for self-expression:

Create environments where individuals feel comfortable expressing their thoughts, feelings, and ideas without fear of criticism or judgment.

Promote creativity:

Encourage others to explore new hobbies, interests, and experiences that can help them uncover their true selves and express their individuality.

Celebrate differences:

Emphasize the beauty of diversity and uniqueness, and celebrate the differences in others rather than trying to conform them to a standard.

Challenge societal norms:

Encourage others to question societal expectations and norms that may hinder their ability to express their true selves and live authentically.

Promote self-reflection:

Encourage individuals to take time for introspection and self-discovery, and provide resources and guidance to help them on their personal journeys.

Lead by example:

Embrace your own individuality and, demonstrate the value of self-discovery, and be open and vulnerable about your own journey to inspire and empower others.

Empower others:

Provide the tools, resources, and support necessary for individuals to cultivate their unique qualities and discover their true identities.

<u>Ways to Unstoppable Empowerment</u>

Embrace your individuality and accept what makes you unique.

Identify your strengths and the qualities that set you apart from others.

Cultivate a strong sense of self-awareness and self-acceptance.

Share your authentic self with others, without fear or hesitation.

Surround yourself with supportive and like-minded individuals who appreciate your uniqueness.

Use your authenticity as a source of empowerment and confidence.

Be open to learning from others and allowing your uniqueness to evolve continuously.

Use your unique perspective to make a positive impact on the world.

Embrace challenges and setbacks as opportunities to showcase your authenticity further.

Be unstoppable in your pursuit of empowerment by embracing your authentic self.

Chapter Summary

- Your story is powerful and can inspire and uplift others.

- Create a supportive and inclusive community to express yourself authentically.

- Advocate for authenticity and self-expression.

- Be a beacon of positivity and hope for others.

- Encourage individuality and self-discovery in others.

FAQ

How can I effectively share my unique design and inner bliss with the world?

To effectively share your unique design and inner bliss with the world, you can start by sharing your personal stories, struggles, and triumphs to inspire and uplift others.

Creating a supportive community of like-minded individuals and advocating for authenticity and self-expression can also help you share your uniqueness.

Being a beacon of positivity and hope for others and encouraging individuality and self-discovery in others are additional ways to effectively share your unique design and inner bliss with the world.

What are some examples of ways to inspire and uplift others through my story?

You can inspire and uplift others through your story by sharing personal experiences of overcoming fears, pursuing passions despite obstacles, or demonstrating resilience and strength in the face of challenges.

For example, sharing how you overcame a fear of public speaking or pursued a passion for art despite financial difficulties can inspire and motivate others in similar situations.

How can I create a supportive and inclusive community?

To create a supportive and inclusive community, you can host events, workshops, or create online platforms to bring like-minded individuals together to celebrate their individuality and unique designs.

Providing a safe space for everyone to express themselves authentically and offering support, understanding, and encouragement can foster a sense of belonging and acceptance within the community.

In what ways can I advocate for authenticity and self-expression?

You can advocate for authenticity and self-expression by speaking out against societal pressures and norms that stifle individuality and by encouraging people to express themselves freely.

This can be done through education, social media, or community activism.

For example, creating campaigns that promote self-love and acceptance or getting involved in organizations that support diversity are effective ways to advocate for authenticity.

How can I be a beacon of positivity and hope for others?

You can be a beacon of positivity and hope for others by embodying a positive attitude and taking optimistic actions that influence others to adopt a more hopeful outlook and remain resilient in the face of adversity.

Simple acts of kindness, gestures of support, and leading by example can all contribute to spreading positivity and hope to those in need.

What are some ways to encourage individuality and self-discovery in others?

You can encourage individuality and self-discovery in others by offering guidance, resources, and encouragement for individuals to explore their passions, interests, and talents without fear of judgment.

Supporting others in their journey of self-discovery and embracing their uniqueness can help them unlock their potential and live more fulfilling lives.

How does sharing my unique design and inner bliss with the world empower me?

Sharing your unique design and inner bliss with the world empowers you by allowing you to inspire and uplift others, create a supportive community, advocate for authenticity, and be a source of positivity and hope for others.

Additionally, encouraging individuality and self-discovery in others also contributes to your own empowerment as you become a catalyst for positive change.

How can I overcome any fears or doubts about sharing my uniqueness with the world?

One way to overcome fears or doubts about sharing your uniqueness with the world is to connect with others who have similar experiences and have successfully shared their own stories and uniqueness.

Seeking support from a community of like-minded individuals and surrounding yourself with positivity and encouragement can help diminish fears and doubts.

What impact can sharing my unique design and inner bliss have on the world?

Sharing your unique design and inner bliss with the world can have a significant impact by inspiring and uplifting others, embracing a sense of belonging and acceptance within a supportive community, advocating for authenticity, spreading positivity and hope, and encouraging individuality and self-discovery in others.

Your authenticity has the power to make a positive impact and contribute to a brighter, more inclusive world.

Now that we've discovered the power of authenticity, let's explore how understanding backward can guide us in making informed decisions.

Life's twists and turns can be easier to navigate when we approach them with insight and perspective.

Navigating Life's Twists and Turns

How Understanding Backward Can Guide Us in Making Informed Decisions

"Life can only be understood backwards, but it must be lived forwards"
— Soren Kierkegaard

- Understand the value of personal growth and development through learning from past experiences and embracing change by recognizing that challenges can provide opportunities for growth.

- Embrace uncertainty and have faith in yourself and your ability to handle whatever comes your way, based on the lessons learned from past experiences.

- Gain a deeper understanding of your values and goals by reflecting on past experiences, using them as a compass to steer your life in a direction that aligns with your values and goals.

- Use the wisdom gained from your past to inform your present and future decisions, ultimately leading to a life that is more authentic and fulfilling.

Blissful Reflection:

The Divine Connection: How One Butterfly Found Strength in the Storms

In a serene village surrounded by nature's undulating canvas, resides an enchanting assembly of butterflies, each fluttering about with their own distinct grace.

Among them is Luna, a butterfly whose wings carry a remarkable pattern that is unique as a signature.

In her early days, Luna's unmatched wings were a source of discomfort, casting a shadow of self-doubt over her sunny existence.

She fluttered under the weight of feeling different and struggled quietly to find her place in the vibrant tapestries of her world.

But as Luna's journey unfolded like the petals of a morning bloom, her perspective began to shift.

She saw that with every passing of the season, she was not just transforming physically but also internally.

Luna's distinctive markings were a metaphor for her singular place in the cosmos, a symbol of her evolutionary gifts.

No longer a mark of alienation, her wings became her anthem, a silent melody to the celebration of divergence.

What once felt like a vulnerability, she now recognized as a symbol of strength.

Yet, the path that Luna fluttered along was not lined with only blossoms and sunshine.

She encountered storms fierce enough to risk her delicate existence and periods of introspection so deep they threatened to engulf her.

During these times, a profound spiritual kinship – a bond unseen but deeply felt – served as her beacon.

Through the chaos, she discovered a sanctuary within herself, a sanctuary built on spiritual pillars that harbored peace and fortified her resolve.

In the eye of the storm, Luna found solace and even enthusiasm in the wisdom that seemed to be whispered to her from beyond the veil.

It was as if she could hear the divine wisdom, encapsulated in the ancient words from 1 Corinthians 2:7-8 NKJV—

"But we speak the wisdom of God in a mystery, the hidden *wis-dom* which God ordained before the ages for our glory, which none of the rulers of this age knew; for had they known, they would not have crucified the Lord of glory."

An intangible clarity that was always there, waiting to be harnessed.

These sacred whispers became Luna's compass, steering her not away from hazards but through them, teaching her that resilience was not just overcoming but thriving through the chaos.

As Luna interacted with other butterflies, each with their own intricacies and tales of rising above, she realized the invaluable role of sharing her newfound insights.

She became a nurturing spirit, speaking life into their struggles, exhorting them to see their unique individuality not as imperfections but as intricate codes etched by life's artistry.

She cited the spiritual counsel from Psalms 32:8-11 NKJV—

"I will instruct you and teach you in the way you should go;
I will guide you with My eye.

Do not be like the horse *or* like the mule,
Which have no understanding,
Which must be harnessed with bit and bridle,
Else they will not come near you.

Many sorrows *shall be* to the wicked;
But he who trusts in the Lord, mercy shall surround him.

Be glad in the Lord and rejoice, you righteous;
And shout for joy, all *you* upright in heart!"

Instilling hope that the wisdom which flows from a higher source can unravel the intricacies of existence, making the unseen palpably guiding.

United in spirit, Luna and her butterfly companions danced on the winds of enlightenment, uplifted by a conviction that their journeys were meant to enrich them with wisdom.

They basked in the presence of the Divine, whose subtle whispers in their hearts now resounded like a mighty chorus, enriching them with peace and a clarity of purpose that transcended their silent flights for they know from 1 Corinthians 2: 12-13 NKJV—

"Now we have received, not the spirit of the world, but the Spirit who is from God, that we might know the things that have been freely given to us by God.

These things we also speak, not in words which man's wisdom teaches but which the Holy Spirit teaches, comparing spiritual things with spiritual."

Their story, woven with the essence of faith, came to reveal a pivotal understanding – that the individuality etched into their being served a higher purpose, a purpose shaped by a celestial choreographer.

Amidst adversities, they held fast to the belief that their intricacies, though seemingly erratic, were orchestrated for a spectacle of glory that only they could showcase.

With time, Luna's fellowship of butterflies began to radiate a magnificence that transcended their physical allure.

Their collective narrative, a mixture of endurance, growth, and transformation, painted an inspiring image.

It asserted the resounding triumph of spirit over circumstance, the splendor of self-rediscovery, and the transformative magic entrusted in owning one's narrative and the divinity that steers it.

For these butterflies, their legacy was etched in the skies, an inspiration to their community and beyond.

Across the distance, whispers of their tale floated, signaling to all the unconquerable power of spirit, the sacred journey of personal evolution, and the alluring liberation found in embracing one's true self and spiritual capacity.

Their journey, a symbol of hope, imprinted on the hearts of many, affirmed that in overcoming trials one's essence is refined and polished.

Luna and her companions had not only found their way through their individual purification but had emerged on the other side with wings that glimmered more fiercely, and more vividly – a testament to the hardship illuminated within them.

Luna's tale, from inception to blossom, offers enlightening insights bathed in a gentle glow.

It imparts the beauty of taking flight amidst life's diversity, of finding solace in one's distinct rhythm, and of triumphing through unity with the spiritual symphony of existence.

Let her story be a tender invitation to spread your own wings, to seek the wisdom that resides within and without, and to glide on the winds of life with courage, harmony, and an unwavering belief in the wonder that is you.

Navigating life's maze often feels like there's no end in sight, but it's the backward glance that offers us the map to find our way out.

The art of self-reflection stands as a beacon of personal growth and development.

When we take the time to peer into the rearview mirror of our experiences, we not only uncover the lessons from our stumbles and stutters but also the wisdom hidden in every turn.

Reflecting allows us to digest our history, to see the patterns in our tapestry of choices, and to distill the essence of wisdom from our missteps.

This introspection is not an exercise in dwelling on the past, but a strategic retreat that empowers us to advance into our future endeavors.

It prompts us to pose the stirring questions that may otherwise go unasked, and it fuels the transformative engine of our personal evolution.

Just as the gardener prunes the branches for a bountiful harvest, we, too, must trim away the overgrowth of our past follies to cultivate a flourishing future.

Simultaneously, embracing the present moment lends a different shade of clarity to our life's canvas.

Mindfulness, the practice of being wholly immersed in the 'now,' is essential for making choices that resonate with our innermost truths.

These deliberate decisions become the brushstrokes of authenticity and intentionality on the mural of our existence.

By grounding ourselves in the present, we cast away the anchors of fear and the nets of regret that often trap us in the undercurrents of life.

We awake to the abundance of opportunities knocking at our door and respond with a heart full of courage and a spirit ready to embrace them.

Understanding our past becomes the compass that guides us, not toward a predetermined destiny, but toward a horizon of possibilities etched with our own hands.

As we shed the weight of bygone errors, we step forward—lighter, lifted by self-assuredness, and propelled by an unwavering sense of purpose.

Here lies the dance of life: a graceful stride into tomorrow, choreographed with the steps we have meticulously learned from yesterday.

Let's dive into the steps to help navigate life's twists and turns.

Step 1: Embracing Growth

Growth is not merely an optional route in life; it's the very essence of our individual journeys.

To embrace growth means you aren't a passive participant in your own story but rather an active architect, passionately willing to sculpt the masterpiece that is your life.

Often, this path requires stepping boldly into the unknown—beyond the familiar walls of our comfort zones.

Imagine the thrill of learning a new language, the exhilaration of mastering a musical instrument, or the satisfaction of completing a challenging hike.

This is the heart of growth—seeking out new experiences that stretch our boundaries and broaden our outlooks.

When criticism comes knocking—instead of raising the drawbridge—welcome it into your castle of self as a royal guest.

Feedback is an invaluable catalyst for development, ripe with the seeds of improvement from which a better self can bloom.

Every moment standing before the mirror of introspection is an opportunity to shape a more refined reflection—a reflection that, day by day, steps closer to the person you aspire to be.

Approach the swirling canvas of life with a brush dipped in the vibrant hue of positivity.

Change, the unceasing river that carves the canyon of our experiences, should not be met with apprehension, but rather with the eager embrace of a dancer, ready to move to its rhythm.

It is in these dances with change that we find ourselves able to twirl into forms of unparalleled personal development and self-improvement.

Life's inevitable zigzags demand not your worry but your wonder, for within their bends lie hidden jewels of wisdom and strength.

For instance, the loss of a job can shatter the ground beneath you, yet from this seismic shift can emerge a mountain of resolve and clarity.

This period of upheaval can lay bare talents previously overshadowed, steer you toward paths unexplored, and gift you the insight to pursue a vocation more aligned with your innermost passions.

To embrace growth is to weave the threads of every experience, be it bright or dark, into the grand tapestry of your evolution.

Celebrate the strength etched into your spirit by adversity, and let the symphony of this celebration resound with the lessons learned and strides taken.

It is in recognizing your own metamorphosis, shaped by life's kaleidoscope of encounters, that you become the symbol of resilience and an inspiration to others on their own path of transformation.

Here are some additional steps:

Reflect on past experiences and identify areas for growth and improvement.

Acknowledge the need for change and be open to new opportunities for personal and professional development.

Set specific and achievable goals for personal growth, whether it's learning a new skill, improving a relationship, or advancing in your career.

Seek out resources and support systems to help facilitate your growth, such as books, courses, mentors, or therapists.

Take ownership of your growth by committing to self-improvement and staying accountable to your goals.

Embrace challenges and setbacks as opportunities, rather than obstacles to be avoided.

Practice self-care and mindfulness to maintain a positive and resilient mindset throughout the process.

Surround yourself with supportive and positive influences that encourage and inspire your personal growth journey.

Continuously evaluate your progress and celebrate your achievements along the way to stay motivated and focused.

Embrace the continual process of growth and development as a lifelong journey, always seeking new ways to evolve and improve.

Step 2: Nurturing Resilience

Reflecting on past setbacks and failures is an essential step toward self-improvement and empowerment.

Each stumbling block we encounter and overcome serves as a testament to our ability to endure and adapt.

The hard times leave us with invaluable lessons, arm us with new skills, and reinforce our resilience.

Sometimes, we find solace and strength in the embrace of friends and family who stand by us when the going gets tough.

Other times, it's the profound discovery of our own untapped well of perseverance that sees us through.

By taking stock of how we've weathered the storms of our past, we learn not just to survive but to thrive.

This accumulated layer of resilience becomes a personal arsenal we can turn to when confronted with new challenges, using our history of resilience as a lever to uplift us during adverse times.

Channeling our resilience involves fostering a positive mindset, one that sees rays of hope within adversity and illuminates the path forward.

When we acknowledge and celebrate the growth that emerges from life's trials, we become beacons of inspiration for ourselves and for others.

It is this spirit that transforms setbacks from perceived disasters into transformative milestones.

By internalizing the idea that setbacks are mere detours on the journey to success, we equip ourselves to approach future stumbling blocks not as insurmountable roadblocks, but as manageable hurdles that we are more than capable of clearing.

Embracing this mindset instills within us the confidence and determination needed to continue pressing forward, turning every challenge into a stepping stone leading to greater heights.

Remember, it's not about the fall, it's about the rise after, and your journey is a living proof that resilience paves the way for victories yet to come.

Here are some additional steps:

Acknowledge the existence of challenges and obstacles in life.

Recognize the importance of building resilience in order to navigate and overcome these challenges.

Understand that resilience is a skill that can be developed and strengthened over time.

Reflect on past experiences and identify times when you have overcome adversity.

Use these past experiences as a source of strength and empowerment.

Cultivate a positive mindset and focus on the potential for growth and learning in the face of challenges.

Seek out support from friends, family, or a therapist to help build resilience.

Practice self-care and prioritize mental and emotional well-being to build inner strength.

Set realistic goals and take small steps toward overcoming challenges.

Embrace failure as an opportunity for growth and use it as a learning experience.

Step 3: Embracing Uncertainty

The journey through life is strewn with crossroads and uncharted waters that often invite uncertainty—an element that is as inevitable as it is unsettling.

Yet, as daunting as it may seem, embracing this uncertainty is an irreplaceable virtue, a touchstone of resilience and grace.

The unknown does not always signal a dark abyss; instead, it can be a canvas stretched out before us, offering a beautiful opportunity for growth, innovation, and self-discovery.

When we release the reins of our need for absolute control, we allow the seeds of spontaneity and flexibility to blossom.

Imagine the relief, the lightness of being that comes from admitting that the future is not ours to see in totality, but is instead a masterpiece being created with each present moment.

Just as an artist trusts the brush strokes to create art, we, too, can trust in the evolving masterwork of our journey.

Reflect on a moment when life's plans unraveled, perhaps taking a direction you had not anticipated or desired.

It is precisely in these instances, when the script of life diverts, that we find the core of our ability to adapt, to grow, and to flourish amidst life's fluctuating tides.

By facing uncertainty with an open mind and heart, we cultivate a freedom to experience life in its fullness, ready to transform every unforeseen challenge into a stepping stone toward self-actualization.

Forsake the instinct to fear what shadows may loom in the ambiguity of what lies ahead; instead, approach each bend in the road with a spirit of curiosity and a heart pulsing with excitement.

To embrace uncertainty is to embrace the essence of living—a testament not to having every answer, but to the determined spirit within that can withstand storms, emboldened by the wisdom of past trials.

Thus, let us step boldly into life's grand tapestry, our eyes alight with the knowledge that we are not the outcome of the paths we choose, but the manner in which we tread them.

Here are some additional steps:

Recognize that uncertainty is a natural part of life and cannot be avoided.

Understand that embracing uncertainty can lead to personal growth and self-discovery.

Reflect on past experiences and acknowledge that we have successfully navigated uncertain situations before.

Develop a mindset of flexibility and adaptability to better manage uncertainty.

Practice mindfulness and grounding techniques to stay present and be less affected by future uncertainties.

Seek support from friends, family, or a support group to share and process feelings of uncertainty.

Focus on what can be controlled and take proactive steps to prepare for potential uncertainties.

Welcome the opportunity to learn and grow from uncertain situations rather than fearing them.

Practice self-compassion and remind ourselves that it's okay to feel uncertain at times.

Embrace uncertainty as a chance for new opportunities and possibilities, rather than something to be feared.

Step 4: Finding Purpose

Reflecting on our past experiences is like sifting through the pages of our own story, finding those chapters that have molded our core.

When we take the time for this introspection, we come face to face with the joyous peaks and challenging depths of our being that have been deeply carved into us.

Each experience holds a key—a key to unlocking the understanding of what brings light to our eyes and accelerates our heartbeat with passion.

The times that tested our resilience aren't just faded memories; they are the rigorous teachers that have fortified our spirit and expanded our boundaries.

To ask oneself which moments have sparked true joy, or which trials have sculpted strength, is to begin tracing the outline of our personal values.

It is this reflective quest that can illuminate the path to a future that thrives on genuine fulfillment and purpose.

With the map of our past in hand, we are poised to plot a course toward a horizon brimming with intention and meaning.

Understanding our values and goals is like setting the sails for a voyage—the clearer the goals, the straighter the journey toward them.

This is where envisioning a life soaked in purpose comes into play.

It's about crafting intentions with the precision of an artist, pursuing opportunities as if they were rare jewels, and aligning our every step with the rhythm of our truest selves.

As we learn to navigate with the compass of self-knowledge, each decision, each ambition becomes a building block of authenticity.

Our purpose becomes our North Star, steadfast and bright, guiding us to not just exist but to live with intention.

Embrace the narrative of your past, for within its lines lies the inspiration to author a future rich with meaning—a future where every step resonates with the heart's deepest aspirations, and life itself becomes an inspired journey of growth and joy.

Here are some additional steps:

Take time to sit and reflect on meaningful experiences in your life.

Identify the moments when you felt most fulfilled and achieved your goals.

Consider the values and beliefs that were present in those moments.

Think about the impact you want to make in the world and what legacy you want to leave behind.

Identify areas of your life where you currently feel purposeful and fulfilled.

Explore any disconnect between your current activities and your desired sense of purpose.

Evaluate your current goals and determine if they are aligned with your values and beliefs.

Consider how you can make changes in your life to live with more purpose and meaning.

Seek out opportunities that align with your values and allow you to make a positive impact.

Create a plan to pursue your purposeful goals and take meaningful steps toward a more purposeful future.

Step 5: Navigating Forward

Navigating forward in life is like steering a ship through open waters, where the insights we gather from self-reflection serve as our compass, directing us toward our desired destination.

Embarking on this voyage requires us to weave our core values and aspirations into the fabric of our daily existence, weaving a tapestry that radiates authenticity and satisfaction.

When we live in harmony with our principles and targets, there's a profound sense of purpose that infuses our actions with meaning.

Each step taken is a deliberate stride toward not just achieving our goals, but also cultivating a life brimming with passion and contentment.

It's the kind of purposeful journey that transforms the mundane into the extraordinary, and the aspirations of yesterday into the achievements of tomorrow.

As we navigate forward with intentionality, we chart a course that not only respects our unique life's purpose but also reinforces our commitment to personal growth and genuine happiness.

To steadfastly navigate through this endeavor, one must embrace the conviction to remain faithful to one's true essence, making choices that resonate with one's deepest convictions.

It is a courageous act to acknowledge the inspiring influence we possess over our destiny and to passionately engage in sculpting the existence we yearn for.

With every reflection and introspection meticulously incorporated into our decision-making, we reap the strength to proceed with assurance and harmony, carving avenues that not only lead to an enriched sense of personal fulfillment but also an amplified sense of intention.

Such empowerment comes from the conscious decision to hold the reins of our lives with unwavering resolve, consistently opting for paths that draw us nearer to our dreams while upholding the integrity of our character.

It is within this dynamic balance of self-awareness and bold action where we find the most profound form of self-expression and the ability to not just exist, but to truly live.

<u>Here are some additional steps:</u>

Identify your values and goals:

Before navigating forward, it's essential to have a clear understanding of what is important to you and what you want to achieve in your life.

Reflect on past experiences:

Take time to reflect on your past experiences, both positive and negative, and consider how they have shaped your values and goals.

Consider different options:

When navigating forward, it's important to consider different options and paths that align with your values and goals.

Seek advice and guidance:

As you navigate forward, don't be afraid to seek advice and guidance from mentors, coaches, or trusted friends and family members.

Make informed decisions:

Use the insights gained from reflection and introspection to make informed decisions that align with your values and goals.

Take calculated risks:

Navigating forward often involves taking risks, but it's important to take calculated risks that align with your values and goals.

Stay flexible:

Life is full of unexpected twists and turns, so staying flexible and adapting to new circumstances as you navigate forward is important.

Stay focused:

Keep your values and goals at the forefront of your mind as you navigate forward, and stay focused on taking actions that align with them.

Embrace change:

Navigating forward may require embracing change and stepping out of your comfort zone in order to grow and progress.

Maintain a positive mindset:

The journey of navigating forward may have its challenges, but maintaining a positive mindset can help you stay motivated and resilient along the way.

Ways to Navigate the Uncertainty:

Acknowledge the uncertainty - Recognize that uncertainty is a natural part of life and be open to embracing it.

Stay focused on the present - Instead of getting caught up in what might happen in the future, concentrate on the current moment and what you can control.

Practice mindfulness - Engage in mindfulness or meditation to help calm the mind and reduce anxiety related to uncertainty.

Set realistic goals - Establish achievable goals and focus on taking small, concrete steps towards them, rather than worrying about the unknown future.

Seek support - Share your concerns with trusted friends, family members, or a therapist to gain perspective and receive support.

Embrace change - Understand that uncertainty often leads to change, and be open to adapting to new circumstances as they arise.

Focus on what you can control - Identify the aspects of a situation that you do have control over and take action in those areas.

Stay informed - Stay updated on relevant information that can help you make more informed decisions amid uncertainty.

Reflect on past successes - Remind yourself of times when you navigated uncertainty successfully and draw confidence from those experiences.

Take care of yourself - Prioritize self-care and maintain healthy habits to help manage stress and build resilience in the face of uncertainty.

Accepting the Past - Acknowledging that we cannot change the past, but we can change how we perceive and learn from it.

Embracing Growth - Recognizing that the challenges and failures of the past have contributed to our growth and understanding of ourselves.

Finding Meaning - Seeking the deeper meaning and lessons within our past experiences, allowing us to move forward with purpose and intention.

Letting Go - Releasing any regrets or resentments from the past, allowing ourselves to move forward with a lighter heart and open mind.

Navigating Life Forward - Applying the wisdom gained from reflecting on our past to navigate our future with intention, confidence, and understanding.

Chapter Summary

- Cultivate gratitude for past experiences

- Embrace personal growth and learning from past experiences

- Embrace uncertainty and have faith in your ability to navigate it

- Use past experiences to find purpose and guide future decisions

FAQ

How can past experiences shape our present and future?

Past experiences can shape our present and future by providing valuable lessons and insights that can guide our decision-making.

For example, if someone faced a difficult situation in the past, such as losing a job, they can reflect on what they learned from that experience and how it helped them grow as a person.

This understanding can then inform future choices and decisions.

Why is it important to cultivate gratitude for past experiences?

Cultivating gratitude for past experiences is important because it allows us to acknowledge the lessons and growth that can come from even the most challenging situations.

By nurturing an attitude of gratitude, we can shift our perspective and find value in every experience, which can ultimately contribute to personal growth and resilience.

What are some strategies for embracing growth and learning from past experiences?

One strategy for embracing growth is to focus on the positive aspects of past experiences, even in difficult situations.

For example, when faced with a setback, consider what was learned and how that experience contributed to personal growth.

This mindset shift can help in seeing the potential for learning and development in every experience.

How can we embrace resilience in the face of adversity?

Embracing resilience in the face of adversity involves recognizing the ability to overcome setbacks and challenges. Reflecting on past experiences and acknowledging how these experiences have contributed to strength and resilience can help in fostering a mindset of inner strength and empowerment.

What is the significance of embracing uncertainty in life?

Embracing uncertainty means having faith in one's ability to navigate through unknowns, based on the lessons learned from past experiences.

It is important to trust that past experiences have prepared us for whatever lies ahead and to approach uncertainty with confidence and resilience.

How can reflecting on past experiences help in finding purpose?

Reflecting on past experiences can help in gaining a deeper understanding of personal values and goals.

By identifying the experiences that have brought joy and fulfillment, individuals can use this understanding to guide them toward a more purposeful future, aligning their choices with what truly matters to them.

What does it mean to navigate forward with intention?

Navigating forward with intention involves using the insights gained from past experiences to inform present and future decisions.

By reflecting on past experiences and using them as guiding principles, individuals can make choices that align with their values and goals, leading to a more authentic and fulfilling life.

What role do values and goals play in navigating life's twists and turns?

Values and goals can act as guiding principles for navigating life's twists and turns, helping individuals make decisions that align with their authentic selves.

Reflecting on past experiences and understanding one's values and goals allows individuals to steer their lives in a direction that is meaningful and fulfilling.

How can embracing growth, developing resilience, and finding purpose help in navigating the uncertainty of the future?

Embracing growth, developing resilience, and finding purpose from past experiences can provide individuals with the tools and mindset to navigate uncertainty with confidence and clarity.

By acknowledging the value in every experience and using these experiences to cultivate inner strength and purpose, individuals can approach the future with resilience and empowerment.

Now that we've learned how understanding backward can guide us, it's time to explore how embracing mistakes can lead to finding clarity in chaos. In this FAQ chapter, "Embracing Mistakes: Finding Clarity in Chaos," we'll delve into practical tips and solutions to turn setbacks into stepping stones.

Embracing Mistakes

FINDING CLARITY IN CHAOS

perseverance inspiration improvement strength confidence performance thoughts learning plan keep trying life success decisions dreams never give up believe try again motivation vision focus desire achievement wishes goals life believe learning career keep on experience dreams life believe confidence learning vision decisions

DON'T GIVE UP

determination attitude life never give up goals courage plan thoughts learning career plan success dedication challenges keep on focus courage attitude knowledge improvement development experience challenges believe learning wishes focus thoughts motivation dreams desire strength direction goals motivation direction

L ife is a journey full of twists and turns, and it's natural to en- counter obstacles and make mistakes along the way.

By addressing these common missteps and FAQs, individuals can learn to embrace their uniqueness and find their own inner bliss, leading to a more fulfilling and joyful life.

Mistake: Not embracing your unique design.

Embracing your unique design means fully accepting and loving yourself just the way you are.

It's important to recognize and celebrate your individuality, and to understand that you have something valuable and irreplaceable to offer the world.

Mistake: Not living with authenticity and intention.

Living authentically means being true to yourself and your values, and making choices that align with your authentic self.

Setting clear intentions for your life allows you to live with purpose and direction, instead of just going through the motions.

Mistake: Not creating a positive mindset.

Developing a positive mindset and attitude is crucial for overall well-being.

It's important to actively seek out and focus on the good in life, and to practice gratitude and positivity even in challenging times.

Mistake: Not finding and living out your true passions.

Living out your true passions brings a sense of fulfillment and purpose to your life.

It's important to identify what truly lights you up and actively pursue those passions, whether it's through hobbies, career choices, or other pursuits.

Mistake: Allowing fear and doubt to hold you back.

Fear and doubt can be paralyzing, preventing you from taking necessary risks and chances.

It's important to acknowledge these feelings but not let them dictate your actions. Instead, focus on building courage and resilience.

Mistake: Neglecting to find balance and well-being.

Finding balance and well-being is essential for living a fulfilling and healthy life.

This can include finding a balance between work and personal life, taking care of your physical and mental health, and prioritizing self-care.

Mistake: Comparing yourself to others.

Comparing yourself to others can lead to feelings of inadequacy and insecurity.

Instead, focus on your own journey and growth, and celebrate the successes of others without feeling diminished by them.

Mistake: Holding onto past experiences and grudges.

Holding onto past experiences and grudges can weigh you down and keep you from moving forward.

It's important to work on letting go of negativity and releasing old wounds in order to move towards a more fulfilling future.

Mistake: Ignoring your intuition and inner voice.

Your intuition and inner voice can be powerful guides in making decisions and navigating life.

It's important to listen to and trust these instincts, as they can lead you towards paths that are aligned with your true self.

Mistake: Focusing solely on external validation.

Seeking validation from others can lead to a never-ending pursuit of approval.

Instead, focus on validating and affirming yourself, and finding internal sources of worth and value.

Mistake: Not setting boundaries.

Setting boundaries is fundamental for maintaining healthy relationships and protecting your own well-being.

It's important to communicate your needs and limits, and to assertively enforce those boundaries when necessary.

Mistake: Not practicing self-care.

Self-care is essential for maintaining overall well-being.

It's important to prioritize activities that nourish and replenish you, whether it's through physical activity, relaxation, hobbies, or seeking support from others.

Mistake: Allowing negative self-talk to dominate your thoughts.

Negative self-talk can be detrimental to your mindset and self-esteem.

It's important to challenge and reframe these negative thoughts, and to practice self-compassion and self-love instead.

Mistake: Avoiding self-reflection and personal growth.

Self-reflection and personal growth are essential for living a fulfilling life.

It's important to evaluate your beliefs, values, and behaviors regularly, and to actively seek out opportunities for growth and development.

Mistake: Not seeking support when needed.

It's important to recognize when you need support and to reach out for help when necessary.

Whether it's from friends, family, or professional sources, seeking support can aid in overcoming challenges and nurturing your well-be

What are some mistakes to avoid when embracing your unique design?

- Comparing yourself to others and feeling inadequate

- Ignoring your own instincts and intuition

- Not seeking out support and guidance from others who understand and appreciate your uniqueness.

How can I avoid making mistakes when finding inner bliss?

- Avoiding negative self-talk and self-criticism

- Don't seek validation and happiness from external sources

- Don't neglect to engage in activities that bring joy and peace

What are common pitfalls to avoid when living with authenticity and intention?

- Compromising your values to please others

- Not being true to yourself and your beliefs

- Allowing fear of judgment and criticism to dictate your actions

What mistakes should I avoid in creating a positive mindset and attitude?

- Allowing negative thoughts to dominate your mind

- Neglecting to practice gratitude and focus on the positive aspects of your life

- Dwelling on past mistakes and failures instead of focusing on personal growth and improvement

How can I avoid making mistakes when finding and living out my true passions?

- Ignoring your interests and passions in favor of societal expectations

- Settling for a career or lifestyle that doesn't align with your passions

- Not taking the time to explore and experiment with different activities and hobbies to discover your true passions

What are some pitfalls to avoid when overcoming fear and doubt?

- Allowing fear to hold you back from pursuing your dreams and goals

- Ignoring opportunities for personal growth and development due to self-doubt

- Allowing fear of failure to prevent you from taking risks and trying new things

How can I avoid mistakes when finding balance and well-being?

- Neglecting to prioritize self-care and personal well-being

- Overcommitting yourself and neglecting to set boundaries in your personal and professional life

- Allowing stress and overwhelm to dictate your actions instead of prioritizing balance and well-being.

What does it mean to embrace your unique design?

Embracing your unique design means accepting and celebrating the qualities, characteristics, and abilities that make you distinctly you.

It's about recognizing and owning your individuality without comparison or judgment.

How can I find inner bliss while embracing my uniqueness?

Inner bliss comes from being in alignment with your true self and finding joy in your authenticity.

You can find inner bliss by practicing self-awareness, self-love, and self-compassion, and by pursuing activities and practices that bring you joy and fulfillment.

What does it mean to live with authenticity and intention?

Living authentically and with intention means being true to yourself, aligning your actions with your values, and being mindful of the choices you make.

It involves being genuine, honest, and transparent in your interactions and living in a way that reflects your true desires and purpose.

How can I create a positive mindset and attitude?

Creating a positive mindset and attitude involves cultivating gratitude, practicing mindfulness, surrounding yourself with positivity, and challenging negative thoughts.

It also includes developing resilience and focusing on solutions rather than dwelling on problems.

How can I find and live out my true passions?

Finding and living out your true passions involves exploring your interests, pursuing opportunities that excite you, and being open to trying new things.

It also requires a willingness to take risks, overcome obstacles, and stay committed to your goals despite challenges.

How can I overcome fear and doubt in pursuing my passions?

To overcome fear and doubt, you can practice self-compassion, develop a growth mindset, seek support from others, and take small steps toward your goals.

It's also helpful to reframe negative beliefs and focus on your strengths and capabilities.

What are some strategies for finding balance and well-being in my life?

Finding balance and well-being involves prioritizing self-care, setting boundaries, establishing healthy routines, and seeking support when needed.

It also requires managing stress, practicing mindfulness, and nurturing your physical, emotional, and mental well-being.

How can I embrace my uniqueness in a society that values conformity?

To embrace your uniqueness in a society that values conformity, you can focus on self-acceptance and self-expression, surround yourself with accepting and supportive individuals, and seek out environments and communities that celebrate diversity and individuality.

What are some practical ways to live with intention and purpose each day?

Living with intention and purpose involves setting goals, prioritizing your time and energy, practicing mindfulness, and regularly reflecting on your values and goals.

It also requires aligning your actions with your intentions and being mindful of how you invest your resources.

How can I cultivate a mindset of abundance and positivity?

To cultivate a mindset of abundance and positivity, you can practice gratitude, focus on abundance rather than scarcity, and choose to see opportunities and potential rather than limitations.

It also involves surrounding yourself with positivity and avoiding negative influences.

How can I discover my true passions and purpose in life?

You can discover your true passions and purpose by exploring your interests, reflecting on your values and strengths, seeking out new experiences, and being open to change and growth.

It's also helpful to seek the guidance of mentors or coaches who can help you gain clarity and direction.

What are some strategies for managing self-doubt and building self-confidence?

To manage self-doubt and build self-confidence, you can challenge negative self-talk, focus on your accomplishments and strengths, seek feedback and support from others, and take small steps outside of your comfort zone.

It's also helpful to practice self-compassion and acknowledge your growth and progress.

How can I find a balance between pursuing my passions and taking care of other responsibilities?

Finding a balance between pursuing your passions and taking care of other responsibilities involves prioritizing your time and energy, setting boundaries, delegating tasks when possible, and practicing effective time management.

It also requires being flexible and adaptable when unexpected challenges arise.

How can I cultivate a sense of well-being and fulfillment in my daily life?

Cultivating a sense of well-being and fulfillment involves engaging in activities that bring you joy and satisfaction, nurturing meaningful relationships, and taking care of your physical, emotional, and mental health.

It also requires finding purpose and meaning in your daily actions and choices.

How can I stay true to myself and my uniqueness in the face of societal pressure and expectations?

Staying true to yourself and your uniqueness in the face of societal pressure and expectations involves staying connected to your values and beliefs, seeking out supportive communities and relationships, and respecting your own boundaries and limitations.

It also requires being assertive in expressing your needs and desires and advocating for your own well-being.

Embracing your uniqueness is a powerful decision that can lead to personal growth and happiness.

When you honor your individuality and listen to your inner voice, you create a sense of authenticity that radiates positivity into every aspect of your life.

This act of self-love is not only beneficial for your own well-being, but it also inspires others to do the same.

By embracing your uniqueness, you become a catalyst for personal growth, and as a result, your inner bliss will unfold, bringing a radiant glow to everything you do.

Honor your inner voice, and watch as your life becomes filled with a newfound sense of happiness and contentment.

Thank you for allowing me to be a part of your journey, and I wish you all the best as you embrace your authentic self and create the life you deserve.

Congratulations!

C ongratulations, you've reached the conclusion of "Conforming Inspiration"!

As you reflect on the insights of this book, remember that embarking on a journey of self-discovery is one of the most remarkable adventures you will ever undertake, and you've already made significant strides.

With the newfound tools and knowledge at your disposal, you are now poised to embrace your authentic self with confidence and grace.

It is within this space of self-awareness and acceptance that you begin to shape a life of purpose and joy.

As you ponder the rich tapestry of insights laid out before you, remember always that the power to manifest positive change is nestled deeply within your being.

Your unique composition, infused with distinctive talents, passions, and experiences, is a gift unto the world.

So, step forth with passion, and don't for a minute shy away from celebrating the vibrant palette of qualities that define you.

To live in alignment with who you truly are is not merely an act of courage but an act of liberation from the chains of inauthenticity.

Now springs forth the moment to transition from contemplation to action, carrying the torch of knowledge into the fields of your daily life.

As you apply these practical, life-altering steps, your mindset will shift; you will start to live more authentically and intentionally.

It's perfectly natural to encounter fear and uncertainty along this path, but recognize these feelings for what they are—stepping stones to greater resilience and wisdom.

When doubt emerges, acknowledge it, lean into it, and let the heat of challenge forge your will as you continue to evolve.

This process is not about blending into the crowd but rather boldly setting yourself apart, unapologetically embracing your unique attributes.

Share your intrinsic gifts with passion, chase your aspirations with steadfast resolve, and craft a life that mirrors the essence of your inner truth.

By doing so, not only will you find personal satisfaction, but you will also serve as a beacon of inspiration, catalyzing a wave of authenticity and empowerment among your peers.

Keep in mind, as you walk this path, your power to sculpt your life's narrative remains unchallenged – your individuality is your superpower, dazzling in its ability to create a life rich with happiness, fulfillment, and purpose.

May you recognize that the quest toward embracing your one-of-a-kind spirit is not a race, but a dance—one that is measured in the rhythm of your personal growth.

So, celebrate each triumph, no matter how small, glean wisdom from the hurdles along the way, and forge ahead with relentless courage and heart.

The world awaits the full expression of your extraordinary essence.

Don't just wear a T-shirt, wear a statement.

Be Blissfully Unique!

embrace Your uniqueness, find Your bliss

Embrace Your Uniqueness with Blissfully Unique T-shirts

Are you tired of blending in with the crowd and conforming to societal expectations? Ready to embrace your one-of-a-kind design?

Look no further! Our Blissfully Unique T-shirts are designed for the bold, the brave, and the blissfully unique. Stand out in a crowd and express your true self with our exclusive 'Blissfully Unique - I am 100% by Design' t-shirts.

Don't just blend in, stand out with Blissfully Unique T-Shirts. Order now and let your true self shine! www.BlissfulTrendz.com

Made with the highest quality materials and featuring eye-catching designs, these shirts are perfect for those who are unapologetically themselves.

Don't just blend in, stand out with Blissfully Unique T-Shirts. Order now and let your true self shine! www.BlissfulTrendz.com

Embrace your uniqueness and celebrate it with pride. Don't just blend in, stand out with Blissfully Unique T-shirts. Order now and let your true self shine!

Each shirt is more than just clothing - it's a symbol of empowerment and a declaration of your commitment to living life on your own terms.

Join the Blissful Trendz community at www.BlissfulTrendz.com and stand out with the power of being 100% by your own design.

Wear it as a declaration of your commitment to living life on your own terms, and encourage others to do the same. Break free from the expectations of the world and love yourself unconditionally.

Don't just wear a T-shirt, wear a statement. Be blissfully unique!

Jesus Saves Souls

No Strife In Life

NO STRIFE IN LIFE

Elevate your wardrobe and nourish your spirit with the "Jesus Saves Souls" inspirational T-shirt from Blissful Trendz.

Designed for those who find strength in their faith and comfort in the knowledge that they're never alone, this shirt is more than a statement—it's a wearable testament to the power of redemption and the lasting love that encompasses us all.

Every design is created with the belief that salvation is within reach and that each of us is a cherished, unique soul in the eyes of the divine. Let this T-shirt be a daily reminder of the tranquility that comes from embracing your spiritual journey, leaving behind the chaos of strife, and finding serenity in life's grand tapestry.

With every wear, you'll inspire not only yourself but also those who cross your path, to seek the bliss that comes from recognizing one's own uniqueness and the purity of a life lived through faith.

Embrace Your Uniqueness and Rewrite Your Story

Are you tired of conforming to societal norms? Ready to embrace your one-of-a-kind design and create a life that reflects your most authentic self? Look no further than "Conforming Inspiration: 7-Step Transformational Pathway to Discovering Your Inner by Design Divine Guidance".

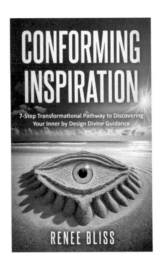

Embrace your uniqueness and tap into your gut instincts - buy "Conforming Inspiration", it will empower you to break free from the constraints of conformity and embrace the truth of who you are. www.Bli ssfulTrendz.com

This book is a powerful guide for unique souls, like you, who are focused on nurturing and developing divine intuition. It will help you understand and trust your inner voice, and rewrite your story. Say goodbye to blending in with the crowd and hello to embracing all the incredible things that make you uniquely you.

Through the 7-step transformational pathway, you'll identify and release limiting beliefs and negative thought patterns, and cultivate a deeper sense of self-love and self-compassion. This is your invitation to find strength, truth, and bliss on your unique journey.

Don't wait any longer to unleash the power of being 100% by your own design. Join the Blissful Trendz community at www.BlissfulTrendz.com and stand out with the power of being authentically you. Your journey to self-discovery and empowerment starts now.

Glossary

Acceptance: The act of embracing and acknowledging your unique design and true self, letting go of the need for approval from others, and finding inner peace in being authentically you.

Adaptability: The ability to adjust to life's challenges and changes with resilience and grace, allowing for the exploration and pursuit of true passions and living with intention.

Alignment: The process of bringing the mind, body, and spirit into harmony with each other and with the universe, allowing for clearer intuition and a deeper connection to divine guidance.

Analytical thinking: The skill of critically examining and understanding your fears and doubts, and overcoming them through positive mindset and attitude, allowing for the creation of a life filled with balance, well-being, and spiritual awareness.

Authenticity: Living and embracing one's true self, thoughts, and emotions, without conforming to societal expectations or pressures.

Awareness: Being fully conscious and attentive to the messages and guidance coming from within and from the universe, to notice the signs and signals that are guiding you toward your highest good.

Balance: Creating harmony and equilibrium in all areas of life, including work, relationships, and personal well-being, in order to achieve a sense of wholeness and contentment.

Being Present: Mentally and emotionally being in the moment, allowing us to truly listen and connect with our inner voice, creating the space to receive divine guidance.

Belief: Having a strong conviction in your unique design and purpose, leading to inner bliss and fulfillment.

Bliss: A state of complete happiness and contentment, achieved by living authentically and intentionally.

Blissfully Unique: Embracing our individuality and accepting our personal journey, empowering our divine intuition and inner voice to guide us in unique ways.

Clarity: Having a clear and lucid understanding of the information and wisdom being received from your intuition, free from doubt or confusion.

Conforming Inspiration: Conforming Inspiration is all about digging deep within ourselves to find that inner transformation. As we unravel the original Greek meaning of 'conform' - Syschematizo - we realize that spiritual conformity isn't just about how we act, it goes beyond our outward behavior. It's a complete makeover inside and out. It's about experiencing inner change that shapes our entire lives. **You've got a choice to make: follow the crowd or let your mind undergo a renewing transformation.**

Contemplation: Reflecting on your core values and goals, leading to a positive mindset and attitude in life.

Core Values: The fundamental principles and beliefs that guide your actions and decisions, helping you find and live out your true passions.

Courage: Overcoming fear and doubt in pursuit of your dreams, leading to a life of fulfillment and purpose.

Creativity: Tapping into your unique talents and passions to bring about positive and inspiring changes, promoting balance and well-being in your life.

Creating a Positive Mindset and Attitude: Cultivating a mindset and attitude that focuses on the good in life, and remains optimistic even in the face of challenges.

Design: Embracing your unique design and finding inner bliss means fully accepting and celebrating who you are, your strengths, talents, and individuality.

Doubt: Overcoming fear and doubt involves recognizing negative thoughts and beliefs, and replacing them with confidence, self-belief, and a positive mindset.

Embracing your unique design and finding inner bliss: This refers to fully accepting and celebrating who you are, and discovering a deep sense of contentment within yourself. It involves embracing your individuality and finding peace within your own skin.

Empathy: Living with authenticity and intention includes understanding and connecting with the experiences and emotions of others, creating meaningful and genuine connections.

Empowerment: Creating a positive mindset and attitude involves recognizing your own worth and capabilities, and taking control of your own life with confidence and strength.

Fear: Finding and living out your true passions means facing and overcoming any fears that may be holding you back, and pursuing what truly brings you joy and fulfillment.

Finding and Living Out Your True Passions: Discovering what truly excites and fulfills you, and actively pursuing those passions in your daily life.

Finding Balance and Well-being: This refers to finding a harmonious equilibrium in all areas of your life, and prioritizing your physical, mental, and emotional health. Striving to maintain a harmonious and healthy equilibrium in all aspects of your life, promoting overall well-being.

Gratitude: The quality of being thankful and appreciative for the unique design and abilities you possess, as well as the experiences and opportunities that come your way.

Growth: The continual process of inner development and self-improvement, embracing your unique design and striving to reach your full potential.

Healthy boundaries: Establishing and maintaining limits that honor your personal values and needs, allowing you to live with authenticity and intention.

Inner: The essence of who you are, including your thoughts, feelings, and beliefs, which should be embraced and nurtured to find inner bliss and fulfillment.

Intention: Deliberate and purposeful action guided by personal values and desires. Living with intention empowers individuals to make choices that align with their unique design and passions, leading to a fulfilling and meaningful life.

Leadership: Taking control of your life and inspiring others to do the same, creating a positive mindset and attitude for yourself and those around you.

Living with Authenticity and Intention: Living in a way that is true to your beliefs, values, and goals, and being mindful and deliberate in your actions.

Meditation: The practice of quieting the mind, connecting with inner peace, and gaining clarity on one's unique purpose and design.

Mindfulness: Being fully present in the moment, embracing one's unique qualities, and finding inner joy in every experience.

Mindset: The attitude and beliefs that shape one's outlook on life, and the ability to shift towards a positive and empowering perspective.

Overcoming: Conquering and rising above feelings of fear and doubt, and moving forward with confidence and determination.

Overcoming Fear and Doubt: This involves facing your fears and self-doubt head-on, confronting and pushing past the self-limiting beliefs and uncertainties that hold you back from reaching your full potential.

Passion: Strong and intense enthusiasm for something that brings joy, fulfillment, and purpose. Discovering and pursuing one's true passions allows for a life filled with purpose and excitement, leading to a sense of personal fulfillment and accomplishment.

Positivity: Maintaining a mindset and attitude that focuses on the good in every situation, and that fosters optimism and hope.

Positive mindset: A mental attitude focused on optimism, gratitude, and resilience. Cultivating a positive mindset enables individuals to overcome fear and doubt, and to approach life with confidence and a can-do attitude.

Reflection: Taking time to contemplate and evaluate one's thoughts, actions, and emotions, and using this insight to align with one's true passions and intentions.

Resilience: The ability to overcome fear and doubt, bounce back from challenges, and stay true to one's authentic self.

Self-Discovery: The process of uncovering one's true passions, embracing one's unique design, and living a fulfilling and purpose-driven life with balance and well-being.

Self-Expression: Fully embracing and expressing your individuality and creativity without fear or inhibition.

Setbacks: Temporary obstacles or challenges that can be viewed as invaluable learning opportunities and catalysts for growth.

Stepping Stones: Small milestones or achievements that lead you closer to your goals and dreams, serving as important markers of progress.

Strength: Personal qualities, skills, and abilities that are unique to you and contribute to your overall success and fulfillment.

Syschematizo (Greek origin): This word refers to a deep internal transformation and renewal, a complete restructuring of our inner selves. This term embodies the process of nurturing and developing our divine intuition, understanding, and trusting our inner voice. It signifies the journey of aligning our thoughts and actions with our intuition and the guidance of the divine. As we syschematizo, we become more attuned to our inner wisdom, allowing it to guide us in making decisions and navigating through life. This process involves surrendering to the wisdom of our higher self and allowing it to lead the way, ultimately resulting in a profound connection with the divine and a more fulfilling and purposeful existence. Let us embrace the process of syschematizo and trust in the power of our divine intuition to transform and guide us.

True: Being genuine and authentic, living in alignment with your core values and beliefs.

Unique: Embracing your individuality and recognizing that there is no one else in the world quite like you.

Well-being: Nurturing and maintaining physical, mental, and emotional health and balance.

Wisdom: Gaining insight and understanding through life experiences, and using that knowledge to make positive, empowering choices.

You: Taking ownership and responsibility for your own thoughts, actions, and well-being.

Made in the USA
Columbia, SC
29 May 2024

36001354R00133